WOMEN WHO HATE OTHER WOMEN

2

Library in Congress Publication Data: TXu 2-094-530

ISBN: 978-0-692088-7-4

Printed in the United States of America

First edition: October 2018

10 9 8 7 6 5 4 3 2 1

In Memorandum and
Loving Memory of
Allen (Louis) Kalik-
The best friend that any
girl could ever ask for
RIP 9/17/50 - 8/14/10

DEDICATION

To everyone that's ever
had a problem with a
female coworker
and lost their job because
of it.
And of course, to my
wonderful Sayreville
students:
It was a pleasure teaching
you and learning from you.

DISCLAIMER

Please note that the information in this book is not meant to be a substitute for legal counsel, therapy, or the rules of your own organization. Please consult an employment law attorney, counselor, or certified workplace coach for such matters.

This book provides general information related to the law. It is not intended to convey or constitute legal advice and it is not a substitute for obtaining legal advice from a qualified attorney. You should not act upon any such information without first seeking qualified professional counsel on your specific matter. I am not a lawyer, and I recommend that you consult one if you want legal advice. It is always advisable to seek legal advice when addressing issues of psychological harassment in the workplace; therefore, readers are urged to use the information contained in this book in a cautious and responsible manner.

The information contained in this book is for general information purposes only. In the event you use any of the information in this book for yourself, the author and the publisher assume no responsibility for your actions. The author makes

AUTHOR'S NOTE

This book is based on extensive
research, in-depth interviews with
women, and incidents I knew of
personally — stories friends had told
me, things I witnessed in the workplace,
and later as a Human Resources
professional. Names have been
changed to protect the innocent and
the guilty. Any similarity to any
particular person or situation is purely
coincidental. All identifying
characteristics were changed, **except**
for my own story.

"Bullying is the sexual harassment of 20 years ago: everybody knows about it, but no one wants to admit it."

–Lewis Maltby,

"Can They Do That?"

PREFACE

I knew that writing this book would be my greatest accomplishment in life. I started this book in 2010, which was undoubtedly the best and the worst year of my life. I'd spent the first half of the year in Paris, only to come back to a never-ending recession. I was uninsured and told I needed hip surgery, my best male friend (Allen) had died of cancer, my Great Uncle had passed away, my BFF and I had ended things, and my soulmate had broken my heart. This book literally kept me going, while I was unemployed and, later, after I moved from New Jersey to Maryland and became housebound due to severe outdoor allergies and inflammation in my body, which resulted in a vicious response from my autoimmune system which triggered chronic fatigue syndrome/systemic exertion intolerance disease, adrenal fatigue, numerous asthma attacks, gluten sensitivity, gum inflammation, loss of teeth enamel, chronic sinusitis, vitamin D deficiency, elevated B-12, elevated neutrophils, hyposmia, fibromyalgia, elevated pulse, orthostatic intolerance, light sensitivity, brain fog, high blood pressure, and possibly mast cell- to name a few. Writing this book helped me keep my sanity when I was at my worst.

What originally prompted me to write this book was a hostess job I had during the recession. The waitresses were horrible to each other. The owners didn't care; they constantly and consistently looked the other way. Coming from the corporate world, I was amazed at what was tolerated in the restaurant industry. Because few people wanted these types of low-paying jobs, restaurants were desperate for employees who would show up on time and do a good job, so they would look the other way while employees hazed other employees. Every day the waitresses would gossip about whomever was off that day. The next day, the person who was previously gossiped about would be welcomed back and someone new, off that day, would be the center of the staff's gossip. This behavior puzzled me.

When I started my research, I would mention to people in passing that I was writing a book. I thought it was an excellent idea. Given that I was a long-term, unemployed person (commonly referred to as a 99er), I had plenty of time on my hands—and plenty of time to write. People would ask me what my topic was. When I'd share my idea with others, I'd either get support or people vehemently against it, claiming this behavior didn't exist and strongly opposed to the book's subject. People would argue with me over my topic. I would get strange looks. I would receive negative responses. People would get defensive. In hindsight, maybe these people were haters themselves (clue: how to spot a hater—someone who says hating doesn't happen). But if that's the case, how come it's happened to me, my friends, strangers, and colleagues? I've also seen it in the workplace, I've dealt with it as a Human Resources professional, I've heard it discussed at Human Resources seminars, I've partaken in discussions with other Human Resources professionals, and there are books available on the subject. Yet people contend it doesn't happen. If that's the case and you don't agree with my book, then I challenge you to write one yourself showing that females are NOT hating on other females in the workplace in the attempt to get them fired or force them to quit. Don't forget to send me a copy! ☺

Perhaps you're wondering where I've worked and in what jobs to have witnessed and experienced hating. Unfortunately, I've had what most would consider "pink collar" jobs, where I was primarily surrounded by women. To put myself through college, I waitressed, and worked in retail. My first professional job was as a high school French teacher. I then went on to work as an administrative assistant, receptionist, hostess (during the recession), and, finally, in Human Resources. From 9-to-5, I was a first-hand witness to drama, only to then go home and listen on the phone to my friends, who would tell me strikingly similar workplace stories. I've worked in various industries throughout New York City, New Jersey, and Maryland.

Perhaps you're wondering if I woke up one morning, took a bitter pill, and decided to sit down and write this book. I'm simply an ordinary person who has seen a lot. I am **not** a professional author, but a writer with something I wanted to say. So, I decided I wanted to write about what I'd seen and heard; I was also compelled to do some research on this topic to get a better understanding of other women who have dealt with the issues explored in these pages. I found way more books on it than I imagined. So, no, this isn't in my head and, no, I'm not a bitter person, nor am I alone in the pain I have experienced. I am but one of many.

It was hard, but eventually I found women willing to share their experiences with me. I posted questions on LinkedIn, which was helpful in getting some feedback. Mostly, though, it was the workplace bullying groups on Facebook that provided me with invaluable feedback. The people I found in these groups felt raw, exposed, bitter, depressed, and powerless, even years after the situation had ended. My thanks to the many people who shared their stories on this painful subject. I know it was difficult for some of you. Thankfully, over the course of writing this book I have seen groups and momentum forming to make hating, bullying, and non-protected harassment illegal. Targets aren't backing down. We are talking and using social media as a platform to open up dialogue. Anybody who has been hated on in the workplace knows how devastating it can be. Women who were not only forced to quit or be fired, but women who had to move, be institutionalized, and go on medical leave, due to the torture they were put through at the hands of their female coworkers; these women are now uniting to shine a piercing light on the troubles they've faced.

This book is meant to be powerful and provocative. If you read it and you're sitting there saying "that happened to me too" or "oh wow" or "exactly" or "oh my goodness" or "that's crazy" or "that's not right", then I've accomplished what I've set out to do. This book is harsh, but it's reality. It's not sugarcoated or meant to be "nice".

Unfortunately, as much as hating exists and is detrimental to its targets, I have no magical solution or list of suggestions that will fix your hating dilemma. If I did, I would most likely be sitting on a tropical island somewhere, not writing this book. So, if you are looking for a great solution that will *solve* your hating dilemma, this is not the book for you. Rather, within these pages, several ways of dealing with a hater are discussed and proposed. There is no cure for this type of behavior.

I am not an expert on this topic. There are tons of people that have researched the issue for years and know a great more than I do. There are also tons of academics and other people who are veritable experts in the field of workplace bullying, just as there are a number of websites dedicated to bullying, harassment, and other workplace issues. However, to my knowledge, this is the only book that deals with the specific subject of women with the intent to get a female coworker fired or to force her to quit. While I applaud the women who have been hated on and were able to stay at their job, this book focuses on women who lost their jobs (fired) or were forced to quit due to their female coworkers.

I don't want what I went through to have been in vain. I'm not a disgruntled former employee of Sayreville War Memorial High School; I just want to tell the truth, which has long been forgotten by most. I want to share my story with the hope that it will educate others. If it could happen to me, it could happen to you.

If you take only three things from this book, I hope they will be this:

1. Some women want to force their female coworkers to quit or get them fired.

2. College doesn't prepare us for what the workplace is really like.

3. Don't ever work for Sayreville School District.

Thank you to everyone who supported me and believed this book would see the light of day. Thank you to all the people that let me interview them, spoke with me, and encouraged me. Your support made an enormous difference.

I would be grateful if you would post a review on Amazon.com. Please like my Facebook author page:

Heather L. Hodsden and join my Facebook group "Keep the Hating Out of the Workplace". Please connect with me on LinkedIn, Instagram, and Twitter. My Twitter handle and Instagram are HHODSDEN.

Please enjoy this book. For my former students: You have in front of you over 300 pages of your former sarcastic, crazy Mademoiselle to bring back fond classroom memories. To all my Facebook friends: You have my glass is half empty, sarcastic, and pessimistic attitude encompassing over 300 pages.

Questions? Thoughts? Comments? Feel free to contact me: **hhodsden@aol.com** **I'm also available for speaking engagements and adjunct opportunities.**

Hating, for the purpose of this book, will be defined as the intentional harmful conduct of aggressive and destructive behavior, which may be hidden or overt, directed at a female coworker by one or more female coworkers over a period of time. It's a form of psychological abuse that can consist of unjustified accusations, general harassment, emotional abuse, and negative words, looks, or gestures. Hating is done with the intention to force the target, voluntarily or involuntarily, out of the workplace by tormenting, belittling, harassing, bullying, isolating, finding fault, wearing down, frustrating, humiliating, intimidating, and manipulating the target. Hating creates a hostile work environment that is so pervasive it forces the target to leave on her own

accord, if she hasn't already been fired.
Most targets find it difficult to escape or
defend themselves and are unsure of
what to do. Hating differs from
bullying and harassment, which may
not necessarily have the goal to get rid
of the target, can involve both genders,
and can be done by a manager or
someone in a superior job position.
Hating may or may not be random;
however, it's not based on someone's
protected class.

TABLE OF CONTENTS

"L'enfer c'est les autres."

(Hell is other people)

-Jean-Paul Sartre,

French Philosopher

and Writer

"Huis Clos"

Introduction

Women Who Hate Other Women focuses on women's issues in the workplace. My goal is to shed light on the problems they face and to tell women's workplace horror stories. This subject, which is extremely close to my heart, has been overlooked, ignored, and ill-addressed. Unfortunately, this topic is real and exists—I know. It's not a myth. It happens all too often. Women are quitting or getting terminated due to their female coworkers. Women are hating on, harassing, sabotaging, destroying, backstabbing, bullying, and gossiping about their fellow female coworkers in an attempt to get them fired or to force them to quit their job. And, unfortunately, they are succeeding.

This book also addresses my belief that we are ill-prepared for the work environment that awaits us. For most, it's not until after spending four rosy years in a learning environment, aka college, where we are nurtured and taught the academic aspect for the career we have chosen. We enter the workforce, with the notion that if we do a good job we will succeed, unprepared that the female sitting next to us may want us gone. After all, as long as one doesn't start problems, one will be okay, right?

The psychological warfare women face at work is difficult to explain to people who have never experienced it. They don't understand. They think it's you, because nothing like that has ever happened to them. If you've never seen or experienced hating first-hand, consider yourself one of the lucky ones.

Hating has been happening for a long time. Women are stealing company time, by wasting it on behavior that doesn't relate to work. In fact, you should almost <u>expect</u> to have problems with your fellow female coworkers when you enter the workforce. The stories you'll read about here will show that it's not men, but women, who ruin each other's careers. These stories are real and can happen to anyone. It's time the truth of what goes on between women in the workplace was put out there.

The goal of this book is to let other women who have been verbally assaulted, fired for no reason of their own, and gossiped about by another female coworker know that they aren't alone. This is an epidemic. It's happening all over — no state, age, race, class, or marital status is immune from it. It could happen to you just as easily as it could happen to the girl in the next cubicle. Maybe next job around you'll be lucky- or maybe not.

"We live and work in a 'gotcha culture'. Whether it's catching a celebrity in a tryst or catching your coworker walking in three minutes late. Some people thrive on the gotcha culture."
-Jim Roache,
Good friend since 1988

Sayreville- My Story

I didn't lose my job because I couldn't teach.

I didn't lose my job because my students hated me.

I didn't lose my job because I had parents who complained.

I didn't lose my job because I couldn't speak French.

I was fired because I was doing a good job. In fact, too good of a job and my female coworkers HATED ME FOR IT!

I wrote this chapter last, as it was the hardest one to write. I put it off, because it's my story. The rest of the book is other people's stories, research, and facts, but this is what happened to me. This is how my female coworkers hated on me and had me terminated. Little did I know that my teaching experience at Sayreville would ruin my teaching career. It's sad how my female coworkers ruined a career that had barely started. It is even sadder that the administration let them. I was young (26) and naïve. I assumed that my female coworkers had my best interests at heart — after all, why wouldn't they? I'm sure to some extent I was in denial. Never did I imagine that I could do my job beyond expectations and still lose it.

During my tenure at Sayreville War Memorial High School, I was harassed, bullied, hazed, ostracized, ganged up on, shunned, intentionally inflicted with emotional distress, humiliated, ridiculed, excluded, insulted, undermined, mentally injured, slandered, isolated (physical and socially), and my character was defamed. On top of it all, I received an adverse employment action: dismissal. I was the target of systematic negative social acts. I was continuously subjected to incidents that the Sayreville administration allowed and didn't put a stop to; that were sufficiently continuous and concerted to alter the conditions of my working environment—all of which created an intimidating, offensive, and abusive work environment. The hating was intentional, severe, recurring and pervasive, and interfered with my ability to perform my job. Sayreville was negligent in taking action to stop the hating I was subjected to, all while I suffered at the misconduct of others. I had no choice but to endure a hostile workplace in order to stay employed. My contract was breached when Sayreville fired me and never investigated my accusations. I didn't realize what was happening to me at the time or that any of this might be illegal or unethical while it was occurring.

My hating story isn't typical, as most don't have witnesses. My hating story, on the other hand, was witnessed by over one hundred students and their parents, not to mention the dozens of teachers who saw what was going on. Yes, I had witnesses. Yes, I complained about my treatment to multiple people. Hell, even my students complained orally and wrote letters. Over a hundred witnesses and nothing was ever done.

I started at Sayreville War Memorial High School in Parlin, New Jersey, in September 2001. On the first day, my students all greeted me with the same monotone un-enthusiasm. They told me that the school didn't want a French department and like the previous eight French teachers, I'd only be there a year. My students were disillusioned, unhappy, frustrated, and all seemed to be having second thoughts about taking French. I told them I was there for the long haul to change things. Eventually my students began to believe in me and trust me. They saw how hard I was working to make French a subject students would want to take, not because of the language requirement, but because it was a wonderful language to learn, a beautiful culture to partake in, and because I was passionate about it. They saw that I cared about them and they appreciated me. I wasn't just their French teacher- I was someone they went to when they needed help, advice, or encouragement. I made a difference in the lives of several of my students while I was there, which I'm glad I got to do. If you think any of this won over the rest of the teachers in my department or the school, it was the complete reverse. I think one of the things that teachers at Sayreville hated about me most was my determination to succeed and my commitment towards turning around the French department.

When I was hired my supervisor told me that he wanted someone to take on a lot of responsibility, take the students to France, revive the program, and get the enrollment numbers up. I did all of that and more. The fact that my dictionary was from 1952 and my textbooks were from the 1970s didn't phase me. I'd spend my free periods photocopying up-to-date materials to give my students the quality education they deserved. There was nothing too good for my students. I continued on with the prior year's French Club, started a French Honor Society chapter there, and began a big sister/big brother program for upper level French students to mentor lower level ones. We went on ice skating trips (very popular in Europe). We got t-shirts with French logos. My students and their parents were grateful. They saw all the hard work I put in and were happy that I was so dedicated to my job. They would hug me at parent-teacher conferences and really got to know me over my two years there. My students said they loved that I cared about them. They'd buy me gifts and give me cards at holidays or when I was sick. My students spoiled me.

I was blessed with great, spirited students who were open to learning, having fun, and my unconventional interactive ways of teaching French. They'd walk into the classroom and I'd be talking loudly in French. They'd laugh. I had only one student cut my class during my two years at Sayreville (which any high school teacher knows is a very low number). People wanted to come to my class. Even students taking Spanish wanted to join the French Club to see what I'd do next. Jumping jacks? Dance and sing? Imitate a dead chicken? Sing poetry? Sing the verb 'être' conjugated to the Mexican hat dance? My students were learning and having fun while doing so. Whether it was eating French cheese, listening to my stories, or looking at pictures of when I lived in France, I knew my students would remember French years later. **I was a great teacher, but I had even better students.**

Teaching, as any good teacher knows, is so much more than just standing up in front of the room lecturing and handing out worksheets. Especially when teaching a foreign language. I kept my students engaged with the lively, energetic, and enthusiastic way I taught them. They were enthralled, enraptured, and on the edge of their seats, always waiting to see what I'd come up with next. We engaged in communicative and interactive activities in the target language. I used games, projects, and songs to develop and reinforce concepts and lower anxiety, thus making second language acquisition input more likely. Students would laugh at each other, while losing themselves in the activities and projects in my class. The fun atmosphere put students more at ease, which was more conducive for learning French. I relied heavily on music to teach my lessons. Music reduces anxiety and inhibition in students learning a foreign language. Whether it was listening to the trendy French rapper Doc Gyneco or singing the French National Anthem "La Marseillaise" — anything involving singing, dancing, or clapping would grab a student's attention even at 7:45 on a Monday morning after a long weekend. Bean bag tosses, Jeopardy, treasure hunts, musical chairs, Scrabble games, Simon Dit, hangman, la maison d'être, French movies, telling stories in French, role playing (my students especially loved to imitate me), verb conjugation relay races, vocabulary bingo, Mardi Gras masks and food, Valentine's Day cards in French, Christmas cards in French, singing Christmas songs "vive le vent", writing poetry, storytelling, Tuesday vocabulary quizzes, Big Momma tests, the fly swatter game, scary stories in French with a flashlight, flash cards, making puppets to tell stories and act out skits for presentations, making posters, cutting out pictures from magazines and labeling them in French — the list goes on. Students were relaxed, laughing, engaged, and having fun- all while learning. Problem was, this got out **AND THE OTHER TEACHERS HATED ME FOR IT.**

For whatever reason, the district had a mentoring policy in place for all new teachers. I was assigned to the most senior Spanish teacher at the school. She'd been there approximately 30 years. Unbeknownst to me, she had a lot of connections. Her sister was the student council advisor and best friends with the district's superintendent. As the sole French teacher, I had lots of plans. However, my mentor, also the Spanish Honor Society advisor, did nothing but discourage me and thwart my plans. While the French program was thriving, my relationship with my mentor and my female coworkers was not. Things discussed between my mentor and I got back to my supervisor, which was not allowed. The mentoring policy at Sayreville firmly dictated that things you discussed between you and your mentor were confidential and not allowed to be repeated, especially to your supervisor. In addition, mentors weren't allowed to comment or have input in your end-of-year evaluation — yet mine did. (This is called a change of policy and procedure.) I soon found out that the rules that applied to all the other teachers didn't apply to her. She didn't have to attend the graduation ceremony or do many other things. My supervisor, being a former science teacher, was clueless and had to rely on my mentor for help. I had an incompetent supervisor who had previously been a science teacher and was clearly in over his head as a world language supervisor. Every time I'd ask him a question, whether it would be on a policy or procedure, he'd tell me he didn't know and to ask my mentor. Even though on paper he ran the department, it was my mentor who actually did.

Each time I did something bigger and better for my students or the French department, my professional career at Sayreville took two steps back. I started to notice a change in most of the other teachers' behavior towards me. I would walk into the faculty room and all the female teachers would stop talking. I was slighted getting invited to the other teachers' after school get-togethers and snubbed during the school day. When I'd greet the math teacher across the hall from me, she'd ignore my hellos. At first, I thought it was just my imagination. Like many victims of hating I was initially confused. Why was I constantly snubbed? Did I do something to bring this on? Why didn't the staff and administration like someone who worked hard, did a good job, and was well-liked by their students? What had I ever done so wrong that the math teacher across the hall would ignore my friendly hellos?

I got these answers from a MALE (NOTE: NOT FEMALE) teacher in the clique. He explained to me that my mentor was jealous over the great job I was doing. She felt that I made her look like she was doing less. (I'm not sure what sort of mental issues or insecurities my mentor had, to perceive my doing well as her doing poorly). Apparently, my mentor had conferred with the Spanish teacher next door to her classroom, incidentally her former student one of the cheerleading coaches, and told her to blackball me. Ah, so that explained where all this was coming from. I did too much. I was committed to my job. I loved my students. I was "different". Because I was hard working and dedicated, I was a threat to others, most specifically to my mentor. Not to mention, I was doing my Masters in French at the most prestigious foreign language university in the United States. I also had youth on my side, as I was over thirty years younger than her. All of which made her hate me and out to get me even more. My mentor campaigned behind my back to ruin my reputation at Sayreville. She caused irreparable damage to my reputation. I often wonder, looking back at that time: Did she go after others before me? Was this the real reason I was the ninth French teacher at Sayreville in ten years?

My mentor put the first nail in my coffin and passed the rest of them out. Once she got the ball rolling she could sit back and relax. It wasn't long before others joined in and "assisted" her in my hating. Thus, commenced the mobbing process to expel me. Others (all female) sporadically joined in: An art teacher, a special education teacher, an English teacher, then another math teacher, then another English teacher, and others. You get the point. The whole "clique" joined forces to expel me from their work environment. I was deliberately never invited to events, even though they were often organized and discussed right in front of me. I was portrayed in a negative light. My social relations were attacked. People talked badly about me. Unfounded rumors were circulated. Misinformation was spread. I was ridiculed. My female coworkers would talk about me, from the fact that I drove a Firebird, dated another teacher there, sang and danced, or anything else they could think of.

My three core haters were my mentor, the cheerleading coach who was the Spanish teacher in the classroom next to her, and the math teacher across the hall from me. They put on a good show for the majority of the staff and administration. Two of my three haters were considered people who contributed to the school. The cheerleading coach presented her good side to the people she knew mattered most. To those she found useful to her career, she was friendly, helpful, and nice. My mentor was considered someone who was honest, sincere, and full of integrity—all which, according to author Patricia Barnes, fall under the definition of a workplace psychopath. My haters were protected due to special relationships of power and connections that they'd established with higher-ups long before I was hired. My mentor was "somebody" within the Sayreville school system. I was no one, so they could easily get rid of me. It's all about power. Knowledge and skills don't guarantee you'll keep your job. Power, however, does.

The hating continued. One day my French 4 class took me aside and said, hey *this is the deal...* They explained to me how the teachers didn't like me and that several had been talking about me and laughing about me behind my back. This confirmed what I'd already heard. They also told me it had been going on for months, but they hadn't known how to approach me. They told me that an English 4 teacher had been talking about how I'd called her on the phone and left her a voicemail, and hahaha, she hadn't called me back and how dare I try to be her friend. She also said that she'd only been nice to me for an occasional ride, as we lived in the same apartment complex. Now my students knew where I lived. What if my students hated me? I wouldn't have wanted them to know where I lived. How unprofessional of my colleagues to talk about me, especially in front of my students.

When I took this job, I was verbally told I'd always have my own classroom as the current classroom had been the French room for over a decade. As any teachers knows, your own classroom is golden. I got my sole classroom, not because I was special, but because there was one designated French room. It had been that way for over a decade and had nothing to do with me. Yet, this too was turned against me as other teachers talked about how I shouldn't, as a first-year teacher there, have my own classroom. Just another negative thing to say about me and blame me for. Another way to attack me. Because I was an excellent French teacher, my coworkers had to resort to making things up, regardless of how ignorant and stupid it made *them* look.

I had great students and not every teacher can say that. Unfortunately, I didn't have great coworkers. I spent my first year there across the hall from and next door to the most horrible coworkers I have ever encountered in my career. It was these same three individuals who jointly went down to the principal, superintendent, and my supervisor to tell them that they refused to teach in the same hallway as me for the next school year. They said they couldn't stand me or my singing and wanted me moved. And like most vindictive, jealous, hating female coworkers they got their way. I was moved out of the foreign language hallway. After all, why *shouldn't* a group of haters control what happens to their target?

One day in May my students, confused, approached me. They said they'd gotten their schedules for next year and that French was in a strange room in the L-wing. I assured them there must have been a mistake. No one had told me the room was being changed. Yet, once again, my students knew more than I did — and before I did. I questioned administration and was told that, yes, I was losing my French classroom and would be in another "room" next year. I use the term *room* loosely here, as it had no windows (I don't even think that's legal for fire reasons) and had been a storage closet (I'm not joking). We couldn't even hear the fire alarm when it went off. Another teacher would have to knock on my door and alert us. I was thrown out of the foreign language hallway and up into a closet in a deserted hallway where no one would come into contact with me unless they purposely went looking for me. I was put in a closet without a PC to check my email even though this was required of us daily, meaning my communication was effectively shut off. I had no heat, only a wall unit air conditioner that never shut off. Yes, my classroom had air conditioning in December, when it was below freezing outside. The air conditioning unit wasn't safe, as more often than not it would throw out ice chips at whomever happened to be near it at the time. Due to the poor air quality, I was sick in September 2002 and four more times before Christmas. I doubt the former closet had undergone an inspection by OSHA (Occupational Safety Health Administration) before becoming my classroom. In short, I was not provided with safe and reasonable working conditions to do my job—and it was putting my students' health at risk.

Obviously, when my three core haters demanded my removal from the hallway there was never any mediation. No administrator voiced their concerns to me or tried to smooth things over. I was pushed out. Yet if my singing and dancing was that loud and bothersome, wouldn't I have been spoken to? Wouldn't my supervisor have asked me to stop? Wouldn't my female coworkers have asked me to tone it down? Had this really been the issue, I'm sure someone would have sat me down and told me to quiet down. When I confronted my supervisor over the accusations that I was purposely moved out of the foreign language hallway he didn't even bother denying it. He admitted that, yes, as long as I was at Sayreville, I'd never teach back in the foreign language hallway again. I have no idea if it's common at

Sayreville for certain teachers to decide what classroom other teachers did or didn't get, but in my case that is exactly what occurred.

I assumed the last month of the school year would end peacefully and without any further mishaps. Gee, what was I thinking? One day a French 4 student, involved in the French Club and the French Honor Society, approached me. She explained that she was on the newspaper and wanted to write an article featuring me and the French department for the last issue of the year. As I was her fourth French teacher, she told me how pleased she was with everything I'd accomplished and implemented to turn the French program around. I was honored and agreed to the interview. She wrote a great article about me and the French program. She even included comments from other students. I was flattered that my students thought so highly of me.

On the day it was published, I could feel the "change" in the foreign language hallway. By third period, reports started to come back to me that my mentor was crying. I glanced at her in between classes and saw her tear-stained face. Later on break, when I asked her what was wrong she became even more upset and refused to tell me. From that point on, my "mentor" refused to speak to me well into the following school year. My supervisor confronted me and told me he'd heard that I'd <u>told</u> a student to write about me and the French program in the newspaper. How on earth would I even know she had a writing assignment? Did he really think I had that much influence over a graduating senior? It was absurd. Who *did* have influence though? Why, my mentor, of course! The following week another "last newspaper of the year" came out. No really! They published an additional issue just to showcase my mentor. I'm sure it won't surprise you to learn that most of the newspaper catered to my mentor and what a great job she was doing in the Spanish department.

On the last day of school in June of 2002, my students hugged me good bye and thanked me for returning. The ones graduating or not taking French the following year, expressed their sadness over not spending another year with me. They told me they wished I'd been their French teacher every year. Even the students that failed opted to redo the class with me instead of switching to Spanish. You would have thought that Sayreville would have appreciated me and been thrilled with everything I was doing to revive the French program. That they would have wanted a teacher going above and beyond what was expected of her. They should have been ecstatic that I had the students engaged, learning, and having fun.

I ended my first year at Sayreville with a bitter taste in my mouth. My supervisor was uneasy whenever he had to interact with me. I'm sure both he and my mentor "assumed" I'd also be another one-year French teacher. If it had happened earlier in the school year, I would have been. However, I was leaving five days after the school year ended for a two-month graduate school French program at the prestigious foreign language school, Middlebury College in Vermont, so spending the summer job searching was out of the question.

I spent the whole summer of 2002 dreading the start of the school year. More often than not, I'd have nightmares about my supervisor, mentor, and the cheerleading coach. I'd wake up disturbed and upset. Even though I felt anxious and depressed the closer it got to September, I was determined to make it work and not let my haters win. So back I went, determined to teach my students French, determined to continue expanding the French program, promote the French language and culture, be the best teacher I could be, and be more involved in the school as an assistant freshman class advisor. I wasn't going to let their hating scare me off. I was there to teach.

My second year there I was friendly to the new teachers. When the cheerleading coach saw this, she too started talking to them. Funny, after that they too started to ignore me. Once again, I was not invited with the other teachers for drinks after work and excluded from conversations, including those that were taking place directly in front of me. Those who were friendly with my haters weren't friendly with me. Even if they didn't attack me, they did nothing—I imagine because they feared going against the flow. Consciously or not, people took sides.

In the fall of 2002, I went to my supervisor with concerns that I was the victim of hating. I told him that several of my female coworkers ignored me, excluded me, weren't friendly, and that one didn't even respond to my hellos. What did he say? He denied it all. He minimized my feelings and dismissed my complaints. He was of no help. In fact, he rescinded our school trip to France. One of the reasons I took this job was the oral promise that I could take my students to France. My supervisor and the administration at Sayreville had a choice- they could intervene and find a solution, or they could join in the mobbing process by beginning the isolation (my room) and expulsion process. They chose the latter.

Two of my classes had more students than desks. Months of complaining never rectified this situation. This forced me to always have a student sitting at my desk. After all, why should administration do something to help me? They'd already made up their minds to fire me. Nonetheless, this didn't deter me or my students. We sang louder, and we spread French throughout the building. We decorated the classroom and hall bulletin boards with pictures from our class parties, Mardi Gras Day, skits, and ice skating trips. Whether it was wearing French t-shirts, fundraising by selling pizza after school, or singing the French National Anthem, my students had spirit. Selling pizza was a great fundraiser and something the students really enjoyed. We raised hundreds of dollars for the French Club. I'm sure we would have raised more money if any of the teachers had bought some. Only *one* teacher ever did. My haters and those who chose to not get involved refused to buy pizza. At first, I thought it was a coincidence, until several teachers told my students they wouldn't buy pizza because they didn't like me. The head freshman class advisor, who was part of the in-crowd, confirmed that the teachers were refusing to buy pizza because I was involved. She also said that the school administration didn't like aggressive females — meaning myself- and didn't take kindly to females who tried to make changes, even positive ones.

At the time, I chose to do nothing but complain to management. I didn't realize what was happening and when I did, I assumed the administration would fix it. Never in my wildest dreams did I imagine I'd be terminated. I should have confronted my haters, but I thought the administration would intervene. So, I complained and I complained and I complained. I complained to my union representatives (yes, I was apparently paying $800 a year in union dues for nothing), Board of Education President, Principal, three vice principals, and my supervisor. The union representative told me they didn't get involved with issues between teachers. The Board of Education President admitted he was aware that there was often hazing among new staff and told me that they hadn't figured out how to handle it. The principal, who was new, didn't want any trouble with his own job, so he went along with what was designated from the superintendent. No one ever investigated my claims. No one ever looked into my accusations. No one ever interviewed my haters. After all, why bother investigating or punishing my haters when they could just terminate me? Problem solved. If I had claimed that I was being sexually harassed or physically assaulted by a female coworker, would the administrators at Sayreville have ignored that too? If my haters were all male, would they have ignored my complaints just as easily?

The only thing that was ever done was for the administration to look for reasons to fire me. It was easier for administrators to pretend I was the issue, to look the other way, and terminate me, rather than investigate my accusations. Management encouraged mobbing by joining in on the hating, thus signifying it was acceptable. Even though my students were doing well and there were no complaints, faults were found. I was portrayed as the problem. As they had no real reason to fire me they had to look for things and make things up. I was excessively monitored. Different standards and policies were used for me than for other teachers. The school decided to make up a new rule — just for me — which was: "If a student and teacher have lunch at the same time, the student isn't allowed to bring their lunch up to the classroom and eat it while they do a make-up test or get extra help". No, really — as they couldn't find anything else, they had to look for what they could and that included making things up by pulling a new policy out of the air just for me. This reprimand, in writing, was the only thing they could think of to put in my file and try to use it to terminate me — how pathetic. I'm not sure what was more stressful — the hating from the teachers or the administration looking for reasons to fire me since there were no real ones. The latter situation became so stressful by January 2003 I was ready to resign, which I told my union representative. I didn't care anymore; I was sick of the hating. The union representative told the principal. The principal said the administration would stop and I would be given a good reference if I stayed until the end of the year (yet another lie). The hating on the administration side let up, but the treatment by the teachers continued.

The unprofessionalism I experienced was so evident to everyone that even my students were aware of it. Even though no administrators or coworkers ever came to my defense, my students did. They wrote letters to the administration complaining about my treatment, how French was viewed overall at the school, and questioned why my mentor was permitted to take her students on a trip to a Spanish restaurant during the school day, but the French class wasn't allowed to go anywhere. My students also complained to their other teachers about how I was treated. It wasn't uncommon for a student to say to me "Mademoiselle I was talking to Mrs. X about you the other day. She feels bad about how the other teachers are treating you." My students felt awful for the way other teachers treated me. It frustrated them to no end. They'd apologize for the other teachers' behaviors and tell me how much they appreciated me.

During the second half of my second year there, I spent the better half of my time crying in front of my students. I was so badly treated by my female coworkers that I could barely function, yet alone teach. I was miserable. The intentional, repeated abuse created an adverse impact on my mental health. It interfered with my work performance and created an atmosphere that was abusive. I started calling in sick every Monday and sometimes Tuesday (absenteeism and reduced productivity are two of the many side effects of hating) to have as long a weekend as possible to recharge and get through the week. I was dealing with the normal pressures and everyday stresses of any teaching job, while trying to maintain my outlook and sanity from the constant hating I was subjected to.

Throughout my second year, I complained to my supervisor numerous times. Again, he did nothing to help me. He only added to my anguish by joining in on the hating. He scheduled me to share a classroom with the cheerleading coach for parent-teacher conferences. He knew she hated me, as she was one of the teachers involved in having my classroom moved. I spoke with a vice-principal, who agreed to help me get my room moved. He was successful in doing so, until my supervisor overrode him and said he wanted me back in the room with her. He knew this would create a hostile work environment. Parents, whose children had been telling them everything, kept whispering to me during the conference that they couldn't believe I was put in the same room as her. One Mom even wrote me a note during the conference—she was that shocked and appalled.

In March of 2003, I was officially told that I wouldn't be rehired for the following year. I was tossed out like leftover cafeteria food. This didn't help my situation. Once my elimination was set in stone there was no reason for either the administration or my coworkers to go to bat for me, be friendly to me, or go out of their way for me. Teachers socially and situationally distanced themselves from me, even more so than before. I was a "social undesirable" excluded from all social gatherings. People no longer spoke to me. No eye contact was made. I was ignored and treated like I had leprosy; I might as well have been invisible. My students were disheartened when they found out I wouldn't be back the following September. Parents offered to go to the board and fight for my job, but I declined. A lot of students decided to not continue with their French studies. French enrollment dropped by approximately 20%. Of course, this too was turned around against me. My supervisor accused me of telling students not to take French. Another lie meant to attack me and portray me in a negative light to justify their treatment of me and the act of firing me.

My supervisor and principal decided to accuse me of only caring about the French program, not the school overall, which was another issue listed on my termination papers. And they decided this because…? There was not one example to support this allegation. Just another lie used to defame my character and justify my termination. This allegation is so general and could have been said about anyone. I can assure you that none of the eight Spanish teachers cared about the French department. Spanish got everything: Lunch trips during the school day, new books, the bulletin board in the foreign language hallway, and they got to choose the winner of the yearly foreign language scholarship. I was the solo French teacher in a department of eight Spanish teachers in a school that clearly favored the latter. Another example? Our in-service day. Now that was a joke. It was divided up by department. I'm sure I attended a great workshop, but I wouldn't know, because all the learning materials were in Spanish.

One of my paid duties, as a class advisor, was to chaperone the junior and senior proms. The teachers in charge (one being the cheerleading coach) decided to exclude me. Yet again, the teachers were running the school, not the administration. When I complained to the principal that my prom chaperone duty had been taken away from me, he brushed me off. It was obvious he didn't care. The head freshmen class advisor chose to not come to my defense, as by then she too had joined in the hating against me. Once again, I was in tears over being excluded, especially over something that was one of my paid advisor duties. I should have confronted the cheerleading coach, who as head senior class advisor had deliberately excluded me from the prom. I almost did, and I wish I had. I'm sure my decision to not confront her was subconsciously due to the lack of support I received from administration.

In May of that year, we had our yearly French Honor Society induction. It was our most important day of the year. The French Club would help set up and sing the French National Anthem. Parents would attend and we'd have food and our induction ceremony. In 2002 my supervisor and **principal** came (note: the **superintendent** would go to the Spanish ones). In 2003, **only** my supervisor came, which once again upset my students and made them feel like French wasn't appreciated. My students surprised me with a bouquet of flowers and a nice speech about how much they would miss me. I was touched. I walked around with these flowers for the rest of the day. By the end of the day, rumors were rampant: I'd allegedly told my students to buy me flowers. Like, really? My supervisor told me that even the principal thought so, whom I had noticed given me an odd look in the hallway.

On my last day at Sayreville I confronted some of my haters. My supervisor stuttered, while searching for his words. My mentor nearly died of embarrassment—she was in tears and had to leave to go home early (really—I'm not making this up!). I would've felt sorry for her- had she not cost me my job. (note: she played the victim role, which emerges when a hater is in trouble. Her crocodile tears were an act to make people feel sorry for her). The cheerleading coach and the math teacher across the hall were nowhere to be found. Luckily, I was resourceful and left them letters in their mailboxes. I was going to have my two cents with them one way or another.

My termination didn't just affect me—it affected my students too. Who suffered in the end? My poor students and the French program at Sayreville. I was the ninth French teacher there in ten years (which should have told me something) and they went back to that pattern. Gone were the pizza sales. Gone was the French Honor Society. Gone were my motivated students. For years to come I'd spend time reading the good ratings my students gave me on www.ratemyteacher.com and the wonderful things they wrote in my yearbooks. Both contained comments from my students about how they felt bad because of the way the other teachers treated me. For 14-year olds to realize how badly my female coworkers were treating me, you know it had to be pretty bad.

I lost my job because my female coworkers didn't like me and wanted me gone. In order to accomplish this, they, with my mentor in charge, complained about me, backstabbed me, gossiped about me, set me up to fail, sabotaged me, and hated on me—among other things. The teachers that got me fired were nasty, miserable, unhappy people who didn't like themselves. They wanted to take their anger out on someone and they did: Me.

Unfortunately, there are plenty of miserable and unhappy teachers out there who stay in teaching solely for the pension and summers off. They count down their twenty-five miserable years with that goal in sight. I never heard so much negativity and complaining at work as I did when I was a teacher. And when they weren't complaining about their students, they were busy stuffing their faces with food. When I left for the corporate world I was surprised that people weren't sitting around the break room openly complaining about their jobs. In the corporate world, you'd get fired for such a thing. In the teaching world you have unions to protect you. Unions that protect you from getting in trouble for hating, harassing, bullying, and mistreating another teacher...

My mentor, the cheerleading coach, and the math teacher all left within the next five years. My mentor took an early retirement the year after my termination. I often wonder if they knew they would be leaving soon if they would have left me alone? Would they have figured I wasn't worth the effort or the time? I can't imagine going to such extremes to get someone fired or force them to quit. Yet, that's exactly what was done to me. I'd feel guilty over someone losing their house or committing suicide or anything else that might occur.

I was the victim of hating with dozens of teachers and over 100 students as witnesses, I was a member of a union, and still I lost my job. I wish I'd known more about workplace hating before Sayreville. I would have been better prepared — mentally and emotionally — and perhaps better able to handle it. I regret not going to the head of personnel, but I had no idea it was an option. No one ever told me to consult a lawyer. I wish I'd known; I probably could have kept my job or gotten a settlement. After another year and a day, I would have been a tenured teacher and secure for life. I left Sayreville when I was 28. I feasibly could have worked there for another 40 years and then perhaps lived another 20 years on my pension. Instead, I'll probably never know job security or retirement in today's economy.

Maybe Sayreville did me a favor by firing me. If they hadn't, I would have stayed and possibly been subjected to hating for many years, or even decades, to come. I couldn't imagine continuing to work there, year after year, and be subjected to hating. One would think that in a school environment, where there are impressionable children, that administrators would go out of their way to make sure there was no hating and that staff behaved professionally at all times. Schools teach that bullying is bad, yet it was "acceptable" for over 100 students to see teachers acting more immature than them and engaging in unprofessional workplace behavior towards another adult.

Sayreville didn't fire me for a legitimate reason. Hell, they didn't even fire me for a job-related reason. My evaluations never showed a performance issue and were always above average. I was fired without cause. I was terminated from Sayreville—not because I couldn't teach, but because there were "issues with staff members". At least that's what it says on my termination paper. I was fired (on paper) for something they couldn't even back up. How could these problems exist, as they were never investigated? It never occurred to me that the hating I endured for almost two years at Sayreville War Memorial High School, which resulted in my wrongful termination, was illegal, morally wrong, and unethical—amongst many other things. It was only many years later, as a Human Resources professional, that I came to the realization that it was.

My two short years at Sayreville War Memorial High School left me with a bittersweet taste for teaching, so I left to enter the corporate world. I assumed that what I had encountered was akin only to teaching—the mentor who ruled as a dictator, the cheerleading coach who still thought of herself as captain of her high school squad, and the miserable math teacher only there to put in her twenty-five years for her pension. Teachers behaving as students and higher ups that were useless, was not what I expected when I went into teaching. Unfortunately, a lot of high school teachers still behave as if they are in high school. All my years of schooling and studying for nothing, as I would never again return to my chosen profession, no thanks to the bad reference my supervisor gave me.

Lesson #1 in life learned: It doesn't matter how good you are at your job- if a female coworker doesn't like you and wants you gone, you'll be gone.

"What I've done, going into a man's world, was tough. You get attacked, but mostly by women. That's the irony. I've found that women are the most competitive and vitriolic. The worst reviews I've gotten were from women...when they're out to get you; they're out to get you."

-Barbara Streisand, American singer, songwriter, actress, and filmmaker

The <u>Real</u> History of Women in the Workplace

The *real* "history" of women in the workplace is to not talk about hating. To avoid discussing any of the negative behavior that women engage in against each other in the workplace. The "history" of women in the workplace is to pretend that "hating" doesn't exist. It's a taboo subject — not something you want to bring up or have brought up around you. The "history" of women in the workplace is to pretend these bad things don't happen. After all, if it hasn't happened to you, then it could never happen, right? If you've never been raped, then it can't happen, right? If you've never experienced racism, then it can't happen, right? If you've never been in a car accident, then it can't happen, right? If you've never been threatened at knife point, then that also can't happen, right? If you've never been fired or forced to quit a job due to a female coworker, then it can't possibly ever happen to anyone else, right? People who <u>have</u> encountered hating haven't talked about it because it's a forbidden topic. Not only will no one believe them, people — even their friends and family — may think they brought it on themselves.

Let's backtrack. In 1964, the US Congress decided that people shouldn't be discriminated against in the workplace based on their race, gender, color, national origin, and religion. Women could no longer be lawfully denied a job due to their gender. Many consider this to be one of most significant legislative employment laws ever passed. Fortunately, Congress continued on with their quest to aid the worker, succeeding in passing laws to prevent discrimination against people with a disability and discrimination based on age. These were followed by the Rehabilitation Act and (GINA) The Genetic Information Nondiscrimination Act, and the Pregnancy Discrimination Act, to name a few. In more recent years, several states have passed laws that prohibit discrimination against someone due to their sexual orientation and/or gender identity. These laws also offer possible legal remedies to targets of hating in the United States who are members of a protected class.

Up until the 1970s, the majority of positions held by women were "pink collar" jobs. They were not careers and they were not front-line positions. The vast majority of women worked in clerical, administrative support, customer service, and entry level management jobs — all typically classified as "pink collar jobs" or common female jobs. They were in essence jobs designed for women. These jobs were thought of as "easy", as a woman's main job and focus was to tend to her home, husband, and kids; thus, these types of jobs didn't take away from her "real one". Women typically held "female" positions such as teachers, secretaries, hairdressers, nurses, waitresses, nannies, housekeepers, and so on. Few served as CEOs or Vice-Presidents, they didn't own their own businesses, and they sure as hell weren't running for President of the United States. The business world catered to men and there was evidence of this nearly everywhere. There were no diaper changing stations or breast pumping rooms in the workplace. Fortunately, the 1970s sparked many changes for women. The Equal Rights Amendment, Title IX, and Roe v. Wade helped to define and clarify women's roles for the future. Each act gave women more rights than they'd ever had before. However, most jobs were still defined by gender—a fact that wasn't questioned. In short, women had little power or say in the business world. They were there, primarily, as support staff—supporting a man, of course.

The 1980s brought about even more changes. Companies started developing sexual harassment policies and in 1986, the first workplace sexual harassment case was heard in the Supreme Court. Until then, most companies had failed to address the issue of sexual harassment, develop policies or training against it, or take action when it was reported, even though the law said they should. Imagine if they had continued to look the other way—most companies would be out of business today. It also became illegal to define jobs by gender. Women started going to college and entering the workforce as prepared young professionals rather, than only in positions designed to support for male professionals. Shocking revelation: They were capable of doing exactly what men had been doing for years, and they often did it better. Women were becoming accountants, doctors, lawyers, engineers, physicists, mathematicians, restaurant owners, business managers, and so forth. Women fought long and hard to earn the right to be treated equally in the workplace. They fought to earn the right to spend 40 hours a week devoting themselves to their chosen profession. Guess what? This may come as a surprise to some, but men and women put their pants on the same way—one leg after the other. Finally, society realized this and equal treatment in the workplace was granted.

Despite the advances women made, the workplace today consists of a hodgepodge of people with a wide variety of backgrounds with different expectations.

Employees aren't unique — they all have their own thoughts, biases, memories, perceptions, way of doing things, and different pasts, which is most likely different than yours. They bring their own baggage and drama into the workplace. Their personality, *not necessarily a good one,* comes into the workplace as well — where it doesn't belong. Everyone is put together for approximately eight hours a day, often in a small uncomfortable space, all for the common cause of work. This means we work with people who didn't choose to work with us and, most likely (unless we did the hiring), with whom we didn't choose to work with either. Due to a number of unfortunate workplace incidents, the government passed laws to try and ensure those eight hours passed more peacefully.

All of this is well and good, but let's talk about what Congress *forgot* to do. (I guess that was just a slight oversight on their part, right?) Congress "assumed" that by passing these laws everyone would go to work happy, perform their jobs, and help each other out. Congress also "assumed" that no female would have it out for another female. Congress "assumed" that females would bond together in the traditionally male-dominated workplace. Congress "assumed" that women would unite and help one another get ahead in the workplace. Congress never thought (or maybe they just weren't thinking at all) that a female coworker might hate on another female coworker for no valid reason at all. Congress never took into account that some people are just plain evil and will do whatever they can to get another person fired or force them to quit.

According to a 2014 survey conducted by the Workplace Bullying Institute (BWI), 27% of American workers reported they were currently being bullied, or had experienced bullying at some point in their careers. A CareerBuilder survey in 2014 found that 28% of workers reported they have felt bullied at work - nearly one in five (19%) of these workers left their jobs because of it. A 2017 scientific poll by Zogby International for the Workplace Bullying Institution Bellingham, WA, showed that 37% of employees are bullied at the workplace- that's 54 million workers! A 2004 survey by the National Institute for Occupational Safety Health (NIOSH) found that, 24.5% of the companies surveyed reported that some degree of bullying had occurred there during the preceding year. In a 2014 CareerBuilder Survey, nearly one-third (32%) reported the bullying to their Human Resources department, but more than half of those who did (58%) said no action was taken. One out of five targets said they didn't report the bully because they feared the bullying would escalate. Yet, this is okay with everyone? *How is any of this okay?*

The statistics get grimmer: According to the HWC (Healthy Workplace Campaign) *bullying is four times more prevalent than illegal discrimination*, yet it's still *legal* in the United States. There are currently no state or federal laws that forbid this type of behavior. Since 2003, 30 states and 2 territories have introduced healthy workplace bills. The proposed legislation would establish a "general civility code" in the workplace that federal law has long sought to avoid. It would give targets a civil right to sue the bully and/or employer for creating a "hostile work environment". Call it hating. Call it harassment. Call it bullying. Call it creating a hostile environment. Hating is many things: Out of line, uncalled for, inappropriate, unprofessional, and psychotic — however, it's not illegal. There's no law that prevents it. It is considered "non-status", because it's not covered by human rights legislation. This makes it harder for targets to sue and gives companies less of a reason to be accountable for their employees' behavior. Hating isn't acceptable or tolerated in most industrialized countries, so why is it okay here? Are females in the USA less valued in the workplace? Why are we so behind in passing a bill to prevent workplace harassment?

At will employment- what I call a joke

Most employees are "at will" and subject to unfair (note use of the word *unfair*) termination in a hating situation. At will employment means either party can end the employment at any time. This means that your employer can terminate you at any time without a valid reason, as long as there isn't a law — such discrimination against race, disability, gender, national origin, religion-violated. Often, workplaces use phrases such as, "it's not working out" OR "you're not a good fit" OR "poor performance" OR "we need someone more experienced" when terminating an employee.

For whatever reason, the United States is the only major industrialized country that has kept the employment-at-will rule. France, Canada, Sweden, Japan, and others have all adopted laws that require employers to show good cause for discharging employees. I'm not sure who this law benefits except lazy managers who don't want to bother putting together a paper trail with a legitimate reason to fire someone.

Arbitration agreements

Even if you're lucky enough to have a company with a hating policy that is actually enforced, that doesn't mean you're in the clear. Recently, companies have taken to using *arbitration agreements*. So, what does this mean? This means that on your first day, or prior to, you were given a stack of papers to fill out, which you most likely didn't read or just glanced at. Hidden within these papers was an arbitration agreement that more or less says that even if your company or coworker blatantly screws you over, you can't take them to court- don't you just love today's modern workplace? In case I need to spell it out for you, an arbitration agreement is in your company's best interests, not yours. The typical arbitration agreement has such verbiage as "This agreement provides that you and **employer's name** mutually agree to resolve specified disputes through arbitration, rather than in court. By agreeing to resolve disputes through arbitration, you and **employer's name** are giving up the right to a court or jury trial on claims covered by the agreement." Basically, you're fucked if your company requires you to sign an arbitration agreement.

Your "fair and impartial" arbitrator is chosen and paid for by your company. Do you believe this person will be fair? And if for some reason she or he does rule in your favor, do you think your company will hire the same arbitrator again? Yes, arbitrators know this going into arbitration. They know that if they make a decision that your company doesn't like, not only will they not be hired by that particular company again, word will get out to other companies that they don't work on the side of the employer. If you're not happy with their decision you're SOL, because in the wonderful agreement you signed, it stated that your arbitrator's decision was final, and you have no right to appeal it.

If your arbitrator does rule in your favor, you can expect to get about half, monetarily wise, that you would have if the case had been tried before a jury of your peers. Juries tend to be more sympathetic and don't owe your company a thing.

Your union (if you have one)

I'm sure you think that your union representative has your best interests at heart. However, like you, they are also an employee of the company. If this isn't a conflict of interest, then I don't know what is. Like our good "friend" the arbitrator, if they go to bat for you, they could wind up on the cutting board too. If you think that companies don't get rid of people they don't like, think again.

Don't get me wrong- unions have their benefits. They're great when it comes to getting raises, bargaining for vacation time, or negotiating for better health insurance. However, the average union representative has no legal background and shouldn't be involved in an employee relations issue. For example, I was a teacher in a union — do you think my union representative told me to speak with someone in Human Resources? No. Do you think my union representative suggested that I consult a lawyer? No. Here I was, in my mid-20s, still wet behind the ears- I didn't know these things. You rely on, and pay, your union with the assumption that the people in it are qualified to help you. Newsflash: Some people get voted into the union, because it's a popularity contest.

If you're in a union and you have an issue with another employee, do most unions refuse to get involved? That I do not know. I only know that in my case my union was beyond useless when it came to providing intervention when I had an issue with my female coworkers.

Human Resources and you- not so perfect together

The goal of Human Resources and managers has been to find, hire, and retain hard working and competent employees. No one ever thought to screen them in terms of their personality. No one thought to ask them interview questions to gauge how they might treat others. If an applicant had experience and seemed qualified, they were considered a good fit. After all, what kind of person would come to work to create drama, hate on others, force people to quit, or set them up to be fired? (Other than a psychopath, that is.) Surely not your average employee. Someone who engages in hating behavior would most likely stand out in the interview process and not get hired, right? And even IF for some reason they got past the initial interview stage and were hired, surely their hating behavior would be immediately noticed, and they'd be terminated, right?

Your hater will most likely have done this before. She'll know how to engage in hating, despite the policies and procedures of the company- if there even are any. She'll be experienced and know how to work around any so-called "rules" your company might have. After all, she doesn't want to lose her job—she wants you to lose *yours*.

Don't be surprised when your hater is all smiles and friendly **IF** (not when) Human Resources interviews her.

After all, she's fine, she's sorry you're not, she hasn't done anything wrong, and, oh yeah, where's the proof that she did? Don't be surprised when your female coworker talks her way out of any inconsistences if management confronts her. She'll have a charming response that will rationalize and explain her behavior.

If Human Resources does conduct an investigation and they agree with you, don't be surprised if she's not fired or punished. Even if Human Resources decides you're 100% in the right, that doesn't mean her manager will let Human Resources terminate her. Even if the hater is caught, managers tend to get protective and defensive of their employees. Especially when the employee has a specific skill or is making money for the company, policies and procedures are often thrown out the window. Unfortunately, haters often stay employed for the wrong reasons — family ties, personal connections, loyalty, or seniority. As a Human Resources professional, I can't tell you how many times I've advised a manger to fire someone and they've refused to — even when the employee has a bad attitude or shows up late or has performance issues. Yet, I've got a manager who won't fire them.

I'd like to tell you that if you **complain** something will get done about your situation, but that would be a lie. I can tell you that from firsthand experience, from things I've seen, from workshops I've attended, from working in Human Resources, from people I've talked to, and from stories my friends have told me. However, this doesn't mean you shouldn't complain — every company, manager, and Human Resources department is different. Maybe someone will go to bat for you. Always remember, **Human**

Resources works for the company, not for you. When you have mutually aligned goals, fine. However, you can't rely on Human Resources to be impartial.

Your company

If you think your company will intervene and make things right, think again. They legally don't have to, so why should they? If you fall into a protected class then they are more likely to investigate, but most likely they will ignore your complaints.

Don't expect your employer to do what's right. Don't expect your employer to care how you are. Don't expect your employer to want, or at least try, to rectify the situation. And don't expect your employer to investigate and punish your hater. The only thing you can "expect" them to do is nothing.

In most cases, nothing is done to resolve hating. This allows management to "get away" by not confronting or directly addressing the hating. When companies look the other way, they accommodate the hater by letting her continue her behavior. When an employee sees that her negative conduct isn't punished, she'll continue her bad behavior. After all, if there are no consequences, why not do what you want? But let's not forget the effect on the target. When management does nothing, it only makes the target become defensive. They know they have only themselves to rely on and that they have to stick up for themselves. Doing nothing practically forces the target to quit.

Even if your company has policies against hating, don't expect things to work in your favor. By going to management and complaining about your hater you risk not only her wrath and retaliation, but also your company's. You're the one who started things by complaining. You're now labeled a troublemaker with too much spare time on your hands. You've complained, and now you risk losing your job.

Junior high — or the workplace?

Is this the workplace or am I back in junior high? Sometimes it's hard to tell the difference. Although more subtle in adults, the hating, bullying, gossiping, harassment, and juvenile behavior that you thought you'd left behind in school continues on in the workplace. Some of our female coworkers were mean girls as children. The only thing that has changed is that they are now meaner as adults. Remember the girl who harassed you, bullied you, made everyone hate you, and not speak to you? The one who made you beg your parents to move so that you could switch schools or beg them to send you to Catholic school (never mind that you weren't Catholic)? Well, she's back — only this time she poses a threat to your livelihood. If you think you've left junior high, think again. Only this time, it's worse, because now we're adults. We should all be acting like adults, but unfortunately, not everyone does. In addition, adults have the capacity to do much more damage to someone than a teenager can. They're smarter, shrewder, and have more resources at hand. The worst is that it's now your job at stake. Your reputation. Your means of living. Half of all Americans live paycheck-to-paycheck. Losing a job over such stupid nonsense can be detrimental to one's sanity, career, and finances. You thought junior high was bad? The queen bee still rules- only this time the stakes are your job.

Defending your comrades- not!

Don't be shocked when your coworkers don't have your back, even those you were friendly with outside of work. They may be appalled over what's happening to you, but don't expect them to stand up for you. Most choose to not get involved, because they feel it's the safest course of action. Even those coworkers who do take your side likely won't speak to management on your behalf. After all, taking your side privately and standing up for you in public are two very different things. If you are somehow successful in filing a lawsuit against your company, don't expect your coworkers to testify on your behalf.

In fact, many of your coworkers may even side with your hater. By taking her side, she won't retaliate against them. Being viewed as your ally could make them next on your hater's list. Standing up for a female coworker who is being poorly treated can cost you more than your job—you might become the hater's next target.

Coworkers who witness hating have three choices: Do nothing, join in, or help the target anyway they can. Witnesses have the most power to stop hating. Unfortunately, most choose to do nothing, especially those who have experienced hating themselves. How do you think that makes the target feel? Lack of support only isolates the target further. Not only is the target dealing with her hater, but she's now lost her workplace "friends". Coworkers' reactions, or lack thereof, can often be more devastating than the hating itself. Even if you have never socialized with these coworkers out of work, you still considered them workplace allies that you could count on; people who would have your back. Now your workplace support system is gone.

Your hater

Your hater will hide her hating from others. Most of the time, she'll hate on you in private where there are no witnesses, so she doesn't look bad. After all, she doesn't want to be prevented from being promoted or lose her job. In public, she'll shower you with compliments and tell you exactly what you want to hear, whether it's true or not. She's a chameleon and has no problem changing color and shape to fit the situation.

Your hater will belittle you and set you up to fail, all with a smile on her face "Oh, you've chosen that outfit to wear to the presentation? Mmmm…well, good luck anyway." Your confidence has now gone out the window as you step into the room to do your presentation. Your hater will do anything she can to put you down and make you look less credible. The bigger the crowd the better. Of course, she'll do it indirectly. She'll be subtle. She won't come right out (at least to your face) and tell you that your presentation sucked. She'll ask, "Why do you think this…?" in a confused tone of voice like you're an idiot child and she's trying to reason with you. Or, "Well, that idea is…interesting", in a way that makes it sound like she's trying to be supportive, but she's really saying that your idea sucks and she feels bad for you — which she really doesn't. When confronted or questioned further, she'll deny that she didn't like your idea. After all, she didn't say that — did she?

In fact, little Miss Innocent has no idea why you think that, and it hurts her feelings. (Victim.)

Your hater will be able to out-maneuver you- after all she's had years of practice. She'll be able to build strong relationships with those in power. She's convincing, has good people skills, and great communication skills. She tells people what they want to hear. She's nice, considerate, friendly, and goes out of her way for others- so why shouldn't they like her? More importantly, why shouldn't they let her do whatever she wants?

Your hater will be manipulative. She'll be able to easily influence others. She's believable and able to naturally manipulate people to see things her way. She'll flatter and pretend to be friends with some of her coworkers, while destroying another coworker at the same time. This confuses coworkers and makes them wonder how someone so nice could ever be capable of hating on someone else. People not on your hater's target list may be clueless. Even people who witness hating may not always understand what's happening. Or why. You can explain it to them until you're blue in the face, but they won't get it. As many haters are smart, charming, and hard workers, their coworkers can't see past that and don't believe that they could ever hate on their fellow female coworkers. Some may even question what the target did to deserve being hated on. Unfortunately, this only constitutes denial and helps the hater get off scot-free.

When your hater's actions are covert, you'll be the last to know that you're her next target. You won't see her coming even if she's at the cubicle next to you. By then it's too late. If you're naïve, good luck working with females.

May I suggest a gender change, starting your own business, or becoming a stay-at-home Mom?

Your hater will play the role of the martyr. She'll pretend that everything she does is in the best interest of the company. It's in the best interest of the company for everyone to hear your business. It's in the best interest for everyone in the company to know what a horrible person you are. Haters act like all they do is sacrifice for the good of the company and, by the way, on her agenda, you're no good for the company. But, hey, sorry, nothing personal, right?

When a female hates on another female, she is out for her own interests, not yours or that of the company. She doesn't care that her hating hurts you, the company, or other employees. She won't let anything, or anyone stand in her way. If she receives information that makes you or any female coworker look bad, she won't hesitate to use it. You lose your job? Oh well, not her problem. You receive a reprimand? She doesn't care. You have a nervous breakdown? Coincidence; it has nothing to do with her. She'll use any means to get what she wants, even if it's underhanded and ruins you. But hey- don't take it personally- she is just doing what's best for her which just happens to be what's bad for you.

If your hater's intent is to destroy you, she'll do anything to achieve her means. Keep in mind that someone sabotaging you is out to get you fired at any cost. She won't stop until you're gone. Voluntarily or involuntarily. Fired or forced to quit, you'll lose your health insurance, your self-worth, integrity, self-esteem, confidence, income, and retirement benefits. Some targets suffer financial losses for years to come. Some even for the rest of their lives. I can identify with the latter.

Committing career suicide

Unfortunately, success in the workplace is largely due to social influence. Sometimes our haters' hold positions of power, not in the sense of job title, but in the sense of influence. Lies and derogatory comments not only have the power to hold someone's career back, but also have the power to have someone demoted, put on probation, and fired. Your workplace success won't be based just on your competence, but also on your interactions with others. No one wants the new Vice-President of marketing to have a checkered past, true or not. No one wants the new head of Human Resources to have had lots of issues with coworkers. "While knowledge, experience, education, and skills certainly contribute to any individual's success at work, it's the quality of an employees' relationships with bosses, coworkers, and clients that will ultimately determine his or her happiness and productivity in the workplace." (Jansen, 2006, p. XIIV).

If you're the target of female hating, your days on the job may be numbered. Once your hater has identified you as her target and realizes that she wants you gone, she'll stop at nothing. She'll start by making sure others, coworkers and management, see you in a negative light. She'll get as many people on her side as possible, especially if she feels like she's been wronged (for example, you got the promotion she wanted, and she's been there longer). The more coworkers your hater involves, the worse the situation becomes. One hater is bad enough, but several?

What your hater says and does **will** affect the way others view you in the workplace. "Recall that perceptions of you by those in power- that is, your reputation- are based on impressions you make. However, if you don't have ready access to those in power (for example, through participation in meetings or by making presentations to upper management), your reputation in their eyes can only be based on reports from others." (Babiak, Paul and Hare, Robert D. p. 300) Your hater may have access to people you don't. She can, and she'll destroy your reputation, unbeknownst to you. My mentor personally knew the superintendent and had access to him. I didn't. She could paint me in a negative light. She could, and she did get me fired. Call me naïve- I had no clue that any of this was going on for most of my first year at Sayreville and the majority of it was happening in the classrooms right next to me.

Is hating for real?

When I first entered the workplace and had the issue at Sayreville, I thought it was just me. I pondered: *What's wrong with me? What am I doing wrong? What do I need to change about myself?* Then I thought that maybe it was just my current job and coworkers who were giving me issues. Eventually, I confided to others what had happened to me. I began to realize that I wasn't the only one having issues with my female coworkers. My friends, friends of friends, coworkers, and fellow students from my Human Resources classes were also having similar issues with their female coworkers. Wow, I thought, it's really not me. I'm not alone. From tattling coworkers to manipulative workplace "friends", women were not looking out for other women in the workplace. Like me, the women with whom I spoke, thought they were the only ones who had experienced this. Trust me: You're not alone, even if it feels that way.

In the past, female workplace conflict was less frequently discussed, as people preferred to live in the land of "it will never happen to me", otherwise known as denial. Those who had experienced it were reluctant to discuss it with those who weren't close friends for fear of being judged. When it happened more than once, women felt embarrassed, ashamed, and fearful of their next job. They stopped revealing their workplace problems to others, even family members, who questioned why they always had these issues. But with more women in the workplace than ever before, this is no longer a hidden shameful subject discussed only behind closed doors. More and more women have stories to tell about how they were fired or forced to quit a job, and how their careers were ruined. Thanks to recent technological advances (such as smart phones and social media) it's even more out in the open. Female workplace conflict is real, even if the subject is deemed as taboo. It exists, whether people want it out in the open or not.

We live in a society that loves drama. Hell, we encourage it. Your work day a little boring? Nothing like watching your female coworker destroy someone. Nothing like some live entertainment to spruce up the workday. Women's rivalry is everywhere (TV, books, Internet, and magazines) and unfortunately, this has carried over into the workplace. "In an analysis of television programs, researchers found that the meanest female characters on television were frequently rewarded for their behavior."

(Simmons, 2011, p. XVII). Working isn't what it used to be. Coworkers are terrible to each other. To some women this type of behavior feels so natural to them that they don't even realize that they're doing it.

Female work relationships today are filled with manipulation, betrayal, undermining, destructiveness, tampering, and hating. Working is like torture when you're backstabbed, manipulated, lied to, and hated on. This type of behavior shouldn't be allowed in the workplace, and yet it is. We tolerate, look the other way, and encourage negative workplace behaviors that would get people fined or even jailed in other countries. We go about our day and consider this behavior normal because it's become so commonplace. Hating is just a normal part of the workday. It's as routine as going through the Starbucks drive thru every morning before work.

The fact that hating persists and that no formal laws exist to deal with and eliminate it makes it seem like it's condoned — almost like it's expected, and that it's allowed. It reinforces that this type of behavior is acceptable. This encourages perpetrators to continue their behavior, especially when they're not punished. This encourages onlookers to join in the negative behavior. Imagine, day after day, going to work in a hostile environment. Unfortunately, some people don't have to imagine it — it's their reality. Work is work; hating needs to stay on reality TV.

Some women feel so trapped by the hating they encounter that they have no choice but to leave their job. How much abuse and misery can someone take? It's not worth it in the end if you're constantly miserable, or is it?

Easier said than done if you have a mortgage and a family to support. Some women have had experiences so bad they've had to go out on medical leave. Some are never able to return to work. Many have sought future work that avoids working with women.

An issue with a female coworker can have a lasting effect on how a woman handles relationships with future coworkers. When you have a negative experience like this with your female coworkers, you can't help but take it with you. You can look forward to starting your new job with paranoia. Some people feel excited over a new job, but former targets of hating start worrying about their new female coworkers: *Will they like me? What can I do to not stand out?* Today's work environment will make you want to downplay your achievements and accomplishments.

No one should ever be embarrassed over losing a job because another woman said or did something to them. You can hold your head up high knowing that you're better than her and that you would never stoop down to her level and her behavior. Of course that being said, that doesn't pay the bills. When Fannie, 38, lost her job due to hating, it took her over a year to find a new one. During that time, she lost her apartment and had her car repossessed. Mean girls, now meaner women, don't realize the consequences their actions can have on someone's life. Or maybe they don't stop to think. Or maybe they do, but they don't care.

After having researched and spoken to several women on this subject, I feel like I've been one of the luckier ones. I never lost a friend over this. My Mother emotionally supported me. I didn't have to endure hating indefinitely. I guess I should thank Sayreville for firing me so I could collect unemployment, before the hating escalated out of control and did even more permanent damage.

I'd like to tell you that the real history of women is that it's great to work with other women. I'd like to tell you that they always have each other's backs, help each other out, want each other to succeed and get promoted, always look out for one another, and would never ever do anything to get another female coworker fired. But if that were true there would be no book for me to write.

The real history is that women are getting other women fired or forcing them to quit. This topic is so taboo people don't talk about it, much less write about it. Women are being terminated NOT due to performance issues, but because of their fellow female coworkers. The real history of women is as follows: There's no rule that says you need to be nice to your coworker or put your best foot forward. Your coworker can treat you like garbage, make you look bad, and yes, get you fired, and this is ALLOWED as long as she doesn't violate a law associated with a protected status. NOW, DOES ANYONE BESIDES ME THINK THIS IS WRONG?

Carissa

Carissa was my neighbor for a year. We continued our friendship after I moved, but eventually fell out of touch. During that time, she was the target of many hating incidents with other females. Carissa was almost 40, thin, attractive, and had never been married—I imagine that brought out the green-eyed monster in more than a few women. In addition, she had the misfortune of choosing jobs that were primarily held by females—teacher's aide, waitress, retail clerk, and administrative assistant. In most cases she opted to quit before she was terminated to save face. Unfortunately, this usually made her ineligible for unemployment.

Two of her hating stories stand out in my mind the most. The first begins when she started her first waitressing job. She was nervous, but she knew she could make great money waitressing. She was determined to go above and beyond what was necessary to succeed in the job. She went out and got books on waitressing. She spent time reading tips on the Internet. She got new clothes (she had to wear black) and even new make-up. Every day she went to work looking fabulous. She memorized the menu before her first day. She would arrive early and sweep up the patio. The owners and manager loved her. She was taking the initiative to get things done and she cared about her appearance. Her customers also loved her. This meant she ended up getting a lot of requests. In short, she was well-liked by her customers and management. Her coworkers? Not so much.

They started ostracizing her. They wouldn't include her in after-work get-togethers, such as Happy Hour. They gave her the silent treatment during work hours. They wouldn't go out of their way to help her, as they would with each other. Then they started stealing her tables and "forgetting" to tell her when she got a new table. One day a table waited for over 40 minutes. Her coworker was "nice" enough to let the manager know. Carissa, of course, got in trouble. She went to the owners and explained to them what was going out. She said she felt like her coworkers didn't like her and were sabotaging her, trying to get her fired. She said they were mean and hostile towards her. The owner and manager who once loved her? Not so much anymore — they didn't want to deal with any issues. They were there to run a successful restaurant, not babysit their employees — especially new ones. Thus, she chose to quit when she saw that not only was nothing being done, but also that management was no longer friendly towards her and she was only getting one shift a week, on the slowest day.

After repeatedly losing jobs due to issues with female coworkers, her friends and family started to realize that it really wasn't her. It was too much of a coincidence when it kept happening. Carissa was sick of it — not knowing what to expect, whom to trust, and getting her hopes up only to have them collapse. She decided to start her own tutoring business. She got a business name, website, business cards, and brochures, and started marketing herself. Unfortunately, it was during the recession. Like most businesses starting up at that time, she realized she would need to do something on the side to supplement her income until her business was up and running full-time. So in to retail she went.

Carissa got a job at a store in the outlets for Christmas season. She liked it. She was happy there. The hours were enough. The location was convenient. The work was easy and pleasant. Her coworkers were somewhat friendly in the beginning. Most of them were there on a part-time basis too. Most worked full-time office jobs, except Carissa. When they asked her what she did she told them that she had a tutoring business. Like most haters, they felt threatened that she owned a business and decided to hate her. They would whisper about her and laugh when she walked into the room or entered certain parts of the store. They ignored her and stopped going out of their way to be friendly. Finally, one had the courage to approach her. She said that everyone had been talking about how she was a liar and <u>didn't</u> own a business. They said if she really DID own a business she wouldn't be working there. Carissa defended herself and went home, but don't think it ended there.

Carissa was scheduled to work two days later. She showed up. All throughout the evening her female coworkers were once again nice to her. Suspicious, Carissa played it low key, which she was right to do. When the evening shift ended she walked to the break room to grab her belongings. Three of her "wonderful" female coworkers were waiting for her with a laptop on the table in front of them. They attacked her. They openly accused her of not having a business and lying about it. They then demanded she show them her website. She happily complied and brought it up on the screen. Dumbfounded, the girls in the room quietly dispersed. Carissa was in shock and upset over the experience. She returned the next day only to receive, once again, the cold shoulder from her coworkers. She quit the following day.

Alexa

I met Alexa one day while I was living in Maryland, over brunch at a meetup. Alexa was young, attractive, intelligent, confident, and had a bubbly personality to boot. She was a positive person and didn't let her recent workplace issue destroy her. She was determined to make the best of a bad situation, which was being unemployed and not being able to collect unemployment.

Alexa was a periodontist. She'd been at her previous position for a little over six years. She was well-liked and well-respected by both her patients and her coworkers. She enjoyed her job and was happy to go there every day. She liked the versatility of her position best. She worked at three different locations. She said it was never monotonous and she was able to interact with more people that way. Her hating situation occurred at her Monday/Tuesday site, which made her dread the weekend, because it would bring her all that closer to Monday. Her coworker, Taryn, had been there for almost 10 years. Taryn worked the front desk and helped prep the rooms. Taryn was knowledgeable about the practice, due to her seniority there. The hating started out slowly, or at least Alexa wasn't aware of it in the beginning, which isn't uncommon. Alexa would be overbooked, or patients wouldn't show, who claimed they had cancelled their appointments. The room preps started getting sloppy—instruments were dirty, things she needed weren't there, or in their usual spot. Then, there were the comments that puzzled Alexa. Was Taryn trying to insult her or just having a bad day? But Alexa had it the day that Taryn mentioned that Alexa had made a mistake on another patient in front of a new patient. This was the first time Alexa had heard of this alleged mistake. Even if it had occurred, it was extremely unprofessional of Taryn to bring it up. So, Alexa went to her site manager, who loved her. She agreed with Alexa that, yes, recently Taryn had changed and not for the better. However, she knew why. Taryn had gone to the site manager recently to explain that she was going through a difficult and painful divorce. The site manager revealed this to Alexa in confidence, as she assumed she would be understanding. Well, okay, Alexa agreed that yes, indeed Taryn must be going through a difficult time. The site manager said she would speak to Taryn about her behavior, as she couldn't be making outbursts in front of patients and doing things that would make the practice look bad. Taryn reverted to her old self — for one week that is.

So once again, Alexa went back to her site manager. Her site manager listened but explained that she had already talked to Alexa about the issue and emphasized, once again, that Taryn was going through a bad time. She told Alexa that she would talk to Taryn again, but said she didn't know what more she could do. She did speak to Taryn. Once again, Taryn altered her behavior, but this time for only three days. This time Alexa went to the manager of all three sites. She said if Taryn didn't stop her behavior that she would like to be transferred. The manager explained that he would speak to the manager at her site and speak to Taryn. He said that there were no full-time openings at the other site and reminded her how she was needed at that site and what a valued employee she was. As I'm sure you can imagine, she didn't feel like a valued employee by that point.

Upper management did discourage Taryn's bad behavior, but they felt sorry for her circumstances and tiptoed around the hating due to her circumstances. The last straw came after an extremely stressful day. Alexa had three no shows and then five people booked for the same slot. She heard Taryn out in the lobby apologizing to the patients and saying that Alexa's personal life was in disarray and that she wasn't performing her best. Alexa stopped what she was doing and walked out to the waiting room. She told Taryn that she wanted to speak with her for a minute. Alexa read Taryn the riot act. She was tired of her games. Who got in trouble? Not Taryn, but Alexa for confronting her. Alexa knew it could be worse, but she couldn't continue to work with Taryn or work with management, who enabled Taryn to continue her behavior. She gave her two weeks' notice. Which, yes, made her unemployed and ineligible for unemployment. Alexa was confident that she would find a new position soon. I hope she did.

Melissa

I found Melissa online. She had a blog, now defunct, about issues with jealous female coworkers. "For the longest time, I could not figure out why my coworkers, all female by the way, would distance themselves from me", was one of the first things she said to me. She went on to explain how she was admittedly naïve and how she believed in working hard and sharing successes. "Never would I have thought that people could be so cold and downright dangerous in their jealousy towards me. It all started with jealous women coworkers and that jealousy tripled when I began to move up in my job and become more successful. Not all the women were jealous but the ladies that were tried to hurt me every day. They would ignore me on purpose, not respond to my hellos, give me nasty glares and stare at me in hateful ways. Whenever they noticed a mistake they would go straight to management and report me and try to get me into trouble. They even went so low as to form a group and email my boss and tell him that I wasn't doing my job. I printed and kept these emails for evidence. It escalated to the point that management, after hearing the numerous complaints from my jealous coworkers, reprimanded me. Sadly, all of the management is female and they seemed to look at me as trouble. I'm now being exposed for little mistakes and even reprimanded for small things that have no bearing on the quality of my work. I'm the highest performer in this business, successful at what I do and now I'm facing a group of jealous coworkers and managers alike that are now mobbing me and try to intimidate me to get me out of the workplace. It's amazing to watch these women, as they are obvious in their task of trying to eliminate me.

Often, when I walk in the door, one of my haters is already waiting for me, ready to harass me before I even start working. I'm facing a jealousy campaign against me," she explained.

"That being said, my life is far from perfect. I'm middle aged, recently divorced, and trying to pay the bills like everyone else. It makes it hurt worse that people are trying to take me down like this and never have I done anything to hurt them. I'm proud of my work and I love my customers. Sadly, my success is one of the things these women, including my managers, must be jealous of. I always try to bend over backwards to please them, only to be met with additional criticism. I have even noticed that they are now moving in on several of my products in this company and trying to sabotage my work by either not ordering work products that I need or plainly removing some of my products from inventory altogether. This is a new low for them. How does one fight this? It is impossible. I'm a hard worker, and heaven forbid I do happen to be attractive too — apparently a lethal combination. I'm not confrontational at all and I prefer to do my work and stay out of their way, but they always find me and try to tear me down. I don't know how to deal with all this negativity but knowing that I'm not alone helps." Melissa had given her two weeks' notice when this book went to print.

"You know Rick you've done me a great service. You've shown me what four years of college didn't teach me- how to play the game and get ahead no matter what it takes."

-Allison Parker, *Melrose Place*

What College Doesn't Teach You

The average female, entering the workplace for the first time, has no idea about the potential drama that can exist between female coworkers. You go to school and do everything right. Then you get a job, but are unable to succeed, because your female coworker has it out for you. College teaches us that if we work hard we will be promoted and get ahead. (Insert laugh here.) No one told us that our female coworkers might influence whether we stay or get ahead on the job. No one told us that the work environment may bring out the worst in our female coworkers. No one told us that our female coworker may be rude, harass us, steal, lie, manipulate, intimidate, bad mouth, cheat, deceive, mislead, and backstab us and that we'd have little to no recourse. No one told us that the workplace may have women insecure in their own jobs who may set out to get you out of yours.

Women entering the workforce may find themselves surprised and disappointed by more than one female coworker. If you expected a workplace where women support one another, you're in for a surprise. In fact, you can expect the exact opposite. You can expect your female coworkers to sabotage you, undermine you, gossip about you, and engage in activities that are detrimental to your career. Whether it's one excuse after another to justify something she's done, showing up late for your meeting, or forgetting to give you the report you've been waiting for. This same "wonderful" coworker will offer to help you pack your desk when you've had enough.

Prior to entering the workforce, we aren't taught about the day-to-day workplace interactions. To my knowledge, there is no class taught in college to warn women to be wary of other women in the workplace. No class on how to deal with women who are out to get other women and force them out of their job. Is it because they don't know? Don't care? Don't believe it? It's never happened to them? So how can one effectively deal with this issue? What if college better prepared us for the workplace conflict we would eventually encounter? What if instead of taking a business elective, we were all required to take a class on how our female coworkers may want us gone. Could this help us be better prepared? Could this help us succeed against our fellow female coworkers and ensure job success?

Unfortunately, you can't always rely on your female coworkers to do what's right, especially what's best for you. I understand that not every female is capable of such heinous acts. In fact, I would like to think that most aren't, but forewarned is forearmed.

College teaches you to be a team player, but what it doesn't teach you is that...

- Your female coworker may use nonverbal communication (looks, silent treatment, gestures) to antagonize you.
- Your female coworker may be a chameleon- some she'll use and abuse, while others she may flatter and cajole.
- Your female coworker may take something you tell her about your personal life and use it against you.
- Your female coworker may do whatever she can to inconvenience you.

- Your female coworker may betray you overnight if she feels that you're in her professional way.
- Your female coworker may do everything and anything she can to make you doubt your competence if she fears your potential. Especially, if her actions make you feel insecure and less confident.
- Your female coworker may take advantage of your kindness and generosity.
- Your female coworker may pretend she has your best interests at heart — *you* just misinterpreted them.
- Your female coworker may try to destroy your good mood with a disparaging remark. After all, she hates to see you happy.
- Your female coworker may do anything she can to damage your reputation. Demeaning comments and offensive remarks in front of others, which damage you beyond repair, are her way of having fun. Especially if it's at your expense.
- Your female coworker may tease you in a passive-aggressive manner. It's her way of saying something offensive without taking responsibility for the damage she's caused. If you call her on it, she may accuse you of not being able to take a joke.
- Your female coworker may do whatever she can to maintain her power in the organization. If it's detrimental to you? Oh well, not her problem.
- Your female coworker may attack you and put you down in public just to look good and be feared.
- Your female coworker may smile to your face, all the while plunging the knife deeper into your back.

- Your female coworker may give you evasive answers to avoid answering your questions and giving you the information you need to do your job. She loves withholding and giving you incorrect information to prevent you from succeeding.
- Your female coworker may publicly challenge your thoughts and opinions, every chance she gets. Her goal is to get the group to agree with her and make you look less credible.
- Your female coworker may try to control you by whatever means are necessary.
- Your female coworker may not get along with you on purpose.
- Your female coworker may send you vague, elusive, and misleading emails that leave you guessing what she really wants.
- Your female coworker may be prone to lying. In fact, she may lie more often than she tells the truth.
- Your female coworker may lack a conscience. After all, if she did have one she wouldn't be capable of all this negative behavior.
- Your female coworker may not share the credit with you. After all, why should she? She wants it all for herself.
- Your female coworker may shift the blame and point the finger at you when something goes wrong. After all, it's never her fault, even when it is.
- Your female coworker may be standoffish or unapproachable when you need her for something.
- Your female coworker may pretend to be your friend, so she can collect information about you to use against you.

- Your female coworker may be a loose cannon. You never know what might set her off.
- Your female coworker may attempt to push your buttons to make you lose it in front of another employee. Her goal is to make you look like a complete idiot in front of your coworkers.
- Your female coworker may bend company rules or go around them to get what she wants. After all, the rules apply to you, not her.
- Your female coworker may not be a team player. After all, she's working towards her own personal goals, not the company's.
- Your female coworker may make "honest" mistakes. When you call her on it, she'll apologize profusely, feign a smile, and tell you it was honestly a mistake.
- Your female coworker may say or do anything she can to diminish your accomplishments and discount your achievements. After all, she prefers to brag about her own accomplishments and achievements so that people can make a fuss over her.
- Your female coworker may prey on your weaknesses to take advantage of you and make herself look good (aka better than you).
- Your female coworker may watch your every move anticipating and hoping you make a mistake. If you do, she'll be quick to point it out to you, but more importantly, to others.
- Your female coworker may share anything confidential you tell her with whomever she feels like.
- Your female coworker may attack you when you're vulnerable (going through a divorce, grieving a loved

one, battling a chronic illness). This is an attempt to draw attention away from her own inadequacies and insecurities.

- Your female coworker may deliberately do things to make you mad and wear on your patience.
- Your female coworker may act defensive when you ask her a question. Note: A defensive coworker is a coworker with something to hide.
- Your female coworker may interrupt you and barge into your conversation before you've finished speaking. After all, what you have to say isn't important, on the contrary, what she has to say is.
- Your female coworker may complain frequently. After all, her problems are your fault.
- Your female coworker may force you to spend less time at your desk and more time hiding from her in the bathroom.
- Your female coworker may gossip about you and slander you by creating lies to make you look bad. She'll be so artful at spreading gossip that no one will be to detect who started it.
- Your female coworker may exclude and isolate you from work-related plans, events, decisions, social gatherings, and conversations. When confronted she'll feign shock. She "forgot". Ignorance is bliss.
- Your female coworker may turn on you for any reason at all. Or no reason at all.
- Your female coworker may steal your spotlight.
- Your female coworker may be nice to you in public but mean in private.

- Your female coworker may criticize you- to your face and behind your back, for little or no reason.
- Your female coworker may make you second guess yourself.
- Your female coworker may send you confusing messages and mixed signals.
- Your female coworker may say and do things that make you cry.
- Your female coworker may tell everyone, including you, that she can do a better job than you.
- Your female coworker may say no when she means yes and yes when she means no.
- Your female coworker may dump her work on you.
- Your female coworker may let you down.
- Your female coworker may give you an up and down scan that says, "I'm judging you".
- Your female coworker may eavesdrop on your private, non-work-related telephone calls. After all, she sees nothing wrong in listening in on your private phone conversations and using what she hears against you.
- Your female coworker may accept your help without a thank you. Just don't expect her to reciprocate, unless she must.
- Your female coworker may insist on doing everything her way.
- Your female coworker may give you unsolicited advice.
- Your female coworker may do your job for you to make you look bad.
- Your female coworker may ignore your contributions at business meetings and functions. After all, what you

have to say doesn't matter- especially since you'll be gone soon.

- Your female coworker may deny all wrong doing if confronted.
- Your female coworker may talk about you as if you aren't in the same room.
- Your female coworker may talk down to you.
- Your female coworker may be jealous of your success.
- Your female coworker may boss you around because she thinks she can.
- Your female coworker may ask you too many questions to disrupt your work. Inappropriate questions at inappropriate times are her specialty.
- Your female coworker may ruin your day, your week, your month, your year. Hell, even your career.
- Your female coworkers may gang up on you like a group of mean girls.
- Your female coworker may openly roll her eyes at you when you leave the room. She does this in the hopes of showing others she doesn't like you and that they shouldn't either.
- Your female coworker may openly accuse you of mistakes you didn't make, especially for the ones she did. After all, you're there to be her scapegoat.
- Your female coworker may act nice one day and then cold the next and then distant the following.
- Your female coworker may pretend to like your ideas if someone else present does. She'll pretend to value your input and your contribution, but only when it's convenient for her.

- Your female coworker may say that you're a team. Unfortunately for you, there's an "I" in <u>her</u> team.
- Your female coworker may tell you that your new idea sucks then pass it off as her own.
- Your female coworker may backstab you all for her own personal gain and professional benefit.
- Your female coworker may "forget" to give you important phone messages.
- Your female coworker may manipulate you to get what she wants. If it makes you look stupid or less credible? Oh well.
- Your female coworker may be happy when you fail.
- Your female coworker may haze you. It will make sorority hazing look like kindergarten play.
- Your female coworker may attack you due to boredom. Attacking you gives her something to look forward to and is the highlight of her day.
- Your female coworker may belittle you and insult you.
- Your female coworker may give you lots of undeserved stress, any and every way she can. You'll carry this stress home with you.
- Your female coworker may be unsympathetic when you have a problem. After all, she doesn't care about your problems or what you have to say.
- Your female coworker may not be willing, when needed, to compromise with you. Compromise? What's that?
- Your female coworker may be insensitive, disrespectful, and un-empathetic.
- Your female coworker may make decisions that involve you without involving you.

- Your female coworker may not go out of her way to accommodate you.
- Your female coworker may not value your time.
- Your female coworker may not keep her word.
- Your female coworker may enjoy seeing you squirm and suffer.
- Your female coworker may make you feel like your thoughts and feelings are insignificant. After all, to her they are.
- Your female coworker may act like you're her rival.
- Your female coworker may be a bitch. Period.
- Your female coworker may demean, anger, and frustrate you.
- Your female coworker may be cruel, self-centered, and uncompassionate.
- Your female coworker's behavior may be highly disruptive while you work, but she won't care. If questioned, she'll find a way to justify it.
- Your female coworker may have nothing better to do than to take her bad day (or life) out on you.
- Your female coworker may abuse and misuse her power.
- Your female coworker may take your stapler, hand lotion, or anything else on your desk, because if it's there it's fair game.
- Your female coworker may not stick up for you and may throw you under the bus again and again and again... (You get the picture)
- Your female coworker may have more negative traits than positive ones.
- Your female coworker may have little to no morals.
- Your female coworker may be angry and moody.

- Your female coworker may judge you without knowing all the facts or hearing your side of the story, especially when she has an audience.
- Your female coworker may shun you for something you may or may not have done.
- Your female coworker may call you names, although usually not to your face.
- Your female coworker may act unprofessional.
- Your female coworker may argue with you. Note: You'll never win.
- Your female coworker may embarrass you.
- Your female coworker may smile at you first thing in the morning and then get to her desk and start actively sabotaging you.
- Your female coworker may be good and convincing at playing the victim, even when she is the perpetrator.
- Your female coworker may encourage people to turn against you.
- Your female coworker may create drama where there is none.
- Your female coworker may not keep her promises.
- Your female coworker may not recognize or appreciate how hard you work.
- Your female coworker may try to paint you in a negative light to other female coworkers.
- Your female coworker may stalk you and spy on you in hopes of learning more information to help you out the door.
- Your female coworker BFF may not rescue you from your hater. She'll fear her wrath and won't want to be next on her list.

- Your female coworker may be inflexible. It's her way or no way at all.
- Your female coworker may be nasty and spiteful just because she can.
- Your female coworker may harm your career in seen and unseen ways.
- Your female coworker may mistreat you so severely that it compromises your health and puts your job in jeopardy.
- Your female coworker may avoid you and stop looking you in the eye when she realizes you may soon be fired.
- Your female coworker may destroy your life. Or at least try to.
- Your female coworker may set you up to get you fired and there may be nothing that you can do about it.

Remember: Forewarned is forearmed. Whose fault is it that we aren't?

Viola

I met Viola when I was doing my Masters in French. I've known Viola for over 15 years. Of Portuguese descent, I'm not exaggerating when I say that with her beautiful olive complexion she could easily pass for someone twenty years younger. Soaking wet she weighs ninety pounds. She's always taken great care of herself — eating organic food and going to the gym. Viola wears only high-end designers, and I don't mean Coach or Michael Kors, neither of which she'd be caught dead in. Viola wears Prada, Gucci, and Dolce & Cabana. Fluent in four languages, Viola's French is perfect.

Since I've known Viola, she has been terminated from approximately eight teaching jobs. Is she a bad teacher? No. Is she late for work? No. Does she mouth off to parents? No. But do her female coworkers hate on her because of her appearance? Yes. At one of her jobs, the administration flat out told her that the teachers were complaining that she only cared about her appearance and not the students.

So, the hating began. Teachers complaining to other teachers, students overhearing. Teachers then started asking students how they were doing in Viola's class, if they were learning, and if they were having issues with her. It doesn't take much to give a middle school kid an idea. After all, if they are doing poorly in a teacher's class and the teacher isn't well-liked by other teachers, then it's probably not their fault, right? Between the teachers making it rough for her and egging the students on, Viola finished out the year without her contract being renewed for the following year. It wasn't the first time it happened, and it wasn't the last.

Carol

Carol took a part-time hostess job to supplement her income one summer. Everyone seemed nice, but she didn't have a lot in common with the waitresses. "They'd been there for ten or twenty years. To me, it was just something temporary." At 35, Carol had a professional job she worked at Monday through Friday.

Carol had a lot in common with the owner of the restaurant. He was also 35 and recently married. "We used to sit and talk about work, the economy, Europe, our travels, college, mutual friends, and numerous other things."

"One waitress, Michelle, got the wrong idea. She went to his wife and told her something was going on between us. Next thing you know, my hours were cut, he was no longer allowed to speak to me, and we were no longer working together. All because of some jealous waitress who felt the need to go to his wife and tell her of her suspicions. Michelle never even asked me if anything was going on. I felt bad for the predicament she put this poor guy in. I can't imagine what kind of strain it put on his marriage."

Carol had never even seen or talked to her boss outside of work. She didn't have his cell phone number and their relationship had always been strictly professional. "I don't know what this woman thought she could accomplish and gain by telling his wife these lies. If we were in a professional office setting, she would have been fired. Michelle put a strain on his marriage and cost me money when I lost hours. I don't know what her motive was — perhaps she was jealous over the amount of time he spent talking to me?" She would later find out they had previously dated, and Michelle was unhappily married and still interested in him.

"What's worse is that his Mom also ran the restaurant and Michelle told his Mom her suspicions. I was mortified- I wanted to quit. When his Mom told me I'd no longer be working on the nights her son worked I wanted to disappear into the earth." Carol knew right then and there she wouldn't be returning the following summer to that job, a job which had become more stress than it was worth.

At the end of the season, Carol went to the Christmas Party the restaurant hosted. However, she hadn't been invited to the cocktail hour; in fact, she hadn't even known about it until she arrived. However, she did come prepared to confront Michelle. After months of working in an atmosphere where people would smile to your face and talk behind your back, she was ready to show that she was not afraid to confront her attacker. However, three things stopped her that night:

- The cashier told her not to stoop down to Michelle's level.
- Management finally gave her the bonus she'd previously been denied.
- Michelle left early before she could act.

Later, Carol mulled over her non-action and regretted not confronting her. She was angry that this waitress thought she could run the restaurant and control who worked there. Much of this was the owners' fault as they let Michelle get away with it.

However, her hater couldn't let things go, even after they no longer worked together. Eight months later Carol started receiving strange texts on her phone. She figured out it was Michelle, who was stupid enough to admit (in writing) that she was going around and talking about her and that she had threatened to get her fired from her new hostessing job at a different restaurant. Knowing it was her, Carol responded. She thanked her for putting everything in writing (wasn't that nice of her?) and told her if she ever heard from her again she'd be contacting a lawyer to sue her for harassment, libel, slander, defamation of character, loss of income, and loss of job. Hopefully, that waitress will think twice before she harasses someone again, no matter who her former lover talks to.

"There's a special place in hell for women who don't help other women."
–Madeleine Albright, Former United States Secretary of State

Mentor- Friend or Foe...?

...or just another female waiting to take you down?

I'm not against mentoring. Personally, I'm all for the mentoring process. I had a bad experience at Sayreville but I also had a great experience, prior to Sayreville, when I worked at Freehold Township for a year. I had a terrific mentor there. I took her kindness for granted and assumed that everyone would treat me as she had. She was kind, soft spoken, encouraging, always available to meet with me, and ready to help me. She took the time to meet with me at least every two weeks, and more often if I had a question. She always sought ways in which she could help. She'd give me suggestions, which as a first-year teacher were quite welcome. She offered to come and observe my class to give me feedback and offered to let me watch her teach her class. She gave me a gift and a hug on my last day there. She was nice, sympathetic, helpful, eager to please me — essentially, everything I could ask for in a mentor. She was a Latin teacher, but was still able to offer me many suggestions I could use as a French teacher.

Mentoring, and a good mentor, is something you can benefit from for decades to come. You can take your valuable learning experience with you, wherever you go. You can gain experience from your mentor's expertise. A mentor can help you grow professionally and personally within the organization. You can use your mentor as a sounding board when you're having an off day. Mentoring can be very fulfilling and extremely valuable to the recipient, mentor, and organization.

Mentoring, when done correctly, can be positive. I've had several unofficial mentors during my career — from members in my local Human Resources chapter, to former bosses, to other people I admired. I think it's a great way to learn and be taught things that you might not learn otherwise.

Mentoring at its finest

Mentoring is defined as a more seasoned employee sharing her/his wisdom, knowledge, and experience to new or less seasoned employee. It's a professional relationship in which a more experienced or more knowledgeable person (known as the mentor) helps to guide and enhance a less experienced or less knowledgeable person (known as the mentorée). The mentor may be older or younger, but have a certain area of expertise. It is a learning and development partnership between someone with vast experience and someone who can learn from that experience. It's a process for the informal transmission of knowledge, specific skills and the psychosocial support perceived by the recipient as relevant to work, career, or professional development. The relationship may be initiated by either party or created through a match initiated by the organization. Mentoring entails informal communication, usually face-to-face, over a set period of time. Afterwards, the pair may continue on in an informal mentoring relationship. The goal of the relationship is to help the mentorée succeed in the organization and field, to teach the mentorée things they might not have otherwise learned, to be a sounding board for the mentorée, and to answer any questions they might have. The relationship crosses job boundaries and becomes personal, usually in a good way. A good mentor will give valuable feedback to help the mentorée improve themselves.

A good mentor will teach the mentorée specific skills and knowledge that are relevant to personal goals. She may also coach the mentorée on a specific skill. She helps the mentorée network by sharing her own connections and resources. The mentorée stands to gain knowledge about the organization's culture and unspoken rules that can be critical for success; as a result the mentorée can adapt more quickly to the organization's culture.

A good mentor will go to bat for you. She'll willingly create visibility for you with upper level management. She'll be your "voice" and sing praises about your performance, potential, and capability to the right people. She can help you grow and cultivate the right opportunities for you.

Organizations usually match people based on functional area or background. Also, any language barriers should be taken into consideration. If someone is from France and English isn't their first language, you might want to assign them someone who speaks both languages.

A new popular way to mentor is called mentoring up. I had an informal mentor, Lola (mentioned in conclusion). When I had a technology question, Lola became my go-to-person. Lola was 15 years my junior. She was a great resource for mentoring upward.

Mentoring gone wrong

Mentoring might not be ideal for everyone. It might also not be ideal for certain people in certain situations. For instance, I personally didn't think I needed a mentor at

Sayreville. I already had my New Jersey teacher's license, I'd taught French for a year, and taught English for a year in France. Imagine if I hadn't been given a mentor? My whole teaching career would have turned out differently.

A negative mentoring experience can have a detrimental impact on your career for many years to come. Your mentor is supposed to protect you, guide you, and offer you support. Not tear you down, gossip about you, manipulate you, harass you, deceive you, ruin your career, and eventually get you fired. If you can't count on your mentor, then who can you count on?

Mentoring, like anything else, can go sour. In which case, you might not be able to turn to your mentor for help and advice like you thought you'd be able to. Your mentor may feel threatened by your success and become resentful. She may block your opportunities for advancement. My mentor at Sayreville was jealous of my success. She didn't have my best interests at heart. She had no intentions of helping me, unless you count helping me get fired.

What if you *do* get a bad mentor? If possible, speak to the person in charge of the mentoring process. You don't have to go into detail. Don't put blame on anyone (unless something has happened and you want her to be held accountable). You can just tell them it's not a good fit and it's not working out. Ask for another mentor. I'm sure you won't be the first person who has and I doubt you'll be the last.

Many people do mentor for the right reasons; however, that's not always the case. At my second teaching job the same foreign language teachers were always mentors and did it solely for the $550 stipend. My fellow former coworker and still friend (let's call her Kathy) had an interesting mentoring experience. Kathy, never one to complain, didn't. Her mentor wouldn't have been around to hear her even if she had. Can you say unavailable? MIA? Kathy met less times with her mentor during three years than I did with mine in a one-month period. Kathy would periodically run into her mentor in the hallway and be asked on the run, "Do you have any questions?" Or "Is everything okay?" Hardly a time to start a conversation with dozens of high school students milling about. Needless to say, Kathy was dismissed after her 3rd year of teaching at that school and chose to pursue a nonteaching career. I often wonder if things would have gone differently for her if she'd had a stronger mentor, like my first one. I'd like to think so.

A mentor/mentorée mismatch doesn't mean any one is at fault- it's just a bad fit. Maybe your organization randomly chooses people who may not have the same background. For instance, should a high school math teacher be mentored by an elementary school art teacher? I'd say no. Companies should engage in surveys to assign people with mutual aligned goals, experiences, and backgrounds. A difference in people's personalities, values, work skills, work schedules, location, and organizational beliefs can have a negative impact on the mentoring process.

You may not always agree on methods, philosophies, or politics, but a solid foundation of trust and respect to mutual professional goals and achievements is what's most important.

My advice:

- Get a mentor. Just because there are some bad mentors out there, doesn't mean you should avoid it. If you get a half-way decent one you're set. Many companies have formal mentoring programs. If your company doesn't have a mentoring program, then unofficially find someone. Sit down at the beginning and outline your professional goals. Make sure you're both on the same page and a good fit. In other words, choose your mentor wisely. You don't want someone who will take credit for your work, blame you for their mistakes, pull rank to get what they want, sabotage you, neglect you, or purposely give you bad advice. Not all of them are bad. A mentor can help guide you and share her own experiences with you. Who knows — she might have already encountered hating and be able to guide you.

- Become a mentor. Take a female under your wings. Share your knowledge, skills, and experience with her. Most importantly, help her avoid and tackle other female coworkers that might be abusing her.

Proceed with caution

Remember: Just because someone has the title of "mentor" doesn't automatically mean they're in your corner. Be wary at first and tread slowly. Say little in the beginning. Feel them out to gauge their intentions. If it's someone you get to choose, choose carefully. Seek informal references within the company if possible. Find someone who can put your best interests first and who is confident enough to want the best for you. If mentoring is mandatory and you're given someone you're leery of, do not trust her and tell her NOTHING. Acknowledge her. Smile. Act grateful. Thank her. Tell her you're fine and have no questions. Then get your questions answered by someone else. Hopefully, you can find an informal mentor to help you. If not, look outside your company to a join a professional organization where you can network and find a "buddy".

If your mentor isn't on your side and willing to go to bat for you, you need to lose them faster than a New York minute.

Janie

Janie had problems with her coworker, Tammie, from the start. For whatever reason they just never clicked. Tammie had been heard on more than one occasion saying that she had nothing in common with Janie, so why try to be nice to her? The main problem was, Tammie was the owner's niece. So, Tammie could do whatever she wanted, which Tammie knew.

Eventually, it became known that Tammie didn't approve of Janie or feel she was a good fit for the company. Janie's boss started avoiding her and wouldn't look her in the eye. She stopped receiving good assignments. Her boss stopped mentioning the future. Her workload slowly dwindled. One Friday evening, her boss took her into her office. Her boss was nice. She apologized and said she had to let her go. She said it wasn't up to her. Luckily, she received a great severance package and managed to find work again almost immediately. Janie was never written up, disciplined, or had a performance issue. She was fired because her coworker with connections wanted her to be gone.

Linda

I connected with Linda, a former nurse at a nursing home, on Facebook. Like so many other targets, Linda was relieved when she was terminated. Her hating was started by a new LPN, who took an instant dislike to Linda for no reason. The LPN's part-time "job" appeared to be getting Linda's coworkers to turn against her. "My coworkers started to report everything I did as if I was God," she told me. They also started distancing themselves from Linda by interacting with her less. Linda thought her hater's behavior was due to the fact that she was well-liked, did a good job, and had seniority. The nursing home wanted a revolving door so they weren't obligated to give raises, which was one reason Linda thinks that they looked the other way when she finally reported the hating.

Linda was otherwise happy there, so she stuck it out. She'd been there for over five years and had never had an issue with another coworker or a complaint from a patient. Her hater had been there for about four months when they finally had an argument. Her hater told her to ignore the doctor's orders and guidelines and to not send a patient to the hospital. She told her to do everything at the nursing home to show that everything had been done before sending the woman to the hospital. Linda refused. Her coworker's response? "Take a mirror and hold it up to your face." The following day, Linda arrived at work only to be suspended. She was shocked and appalled as she had no idea why. No explanation was given to her. The only thing she was told was that the administrator would call her. She waited, but he never did. When someone finally reached out to her, it was to inform her that there had been several complaints from patients and family members and that her job performance was subpar. "Really? I was given a raise and you told me you had received a lot of praise about me", she responded. Although it was never confirmed, Linda assumed her hater had a friend at the top, because when it came down to it she won — all Linda's loyalty and years of service meant nothing.

"The pressure that women face to 'have it all' almost encourages women to go after whatever they want, even if it means stepping on others."
-Wilhelmina Slater, *Ugly Betty*

Why? Why? Why?

Why do women hate on other women? Because they can. And most of the time they get away with it. Even when they don't, the consequences are usually very small. If you knew that tomorrow you could walk into a Louis Vuitton store and steal as many handbags as you'd like and there would be no repercussions, would you do it? Knowing that it was immoral and unethical to steal, would you do it anyway? Just think—no punishment and you can own a Louis! Some might and some might not. Well, the same applies to women hating on other women.

For decades, women have been sabotaging, backstabbing, bullying, and hating on other women in the workplace. Friend or foe, if you're a woman, beware. Nothing is off limits to a woman who wants you gone. But why? Why do women set out to get another woman fired or force her to quit? Your position, jealousy, they are bored, the workplace tolerates it, they think it's fun, they think it'll make them popular, they think it will make them feared, they hate you, for the thrill, they are mentally unstable, you have something they want, it makes them feel powerful, they want to be in control, they are envious, they are haters? All of the above? None of the above? Whatever the reason, haters want nothing better than to bring about your downfall.

Many authors and psychologists feel that women's issues in the workplace stem from competition, envy, and jealousy. I agree, but I feel that those aren't, by far, the only reasons. I don't think there's any one answer. I think it depends on the individual and the specific situation. There are many underlying issues that trigger these feelings, but whatever it is, it is negativity and doesn't belong in the workplace. However, I think the main reason is that they can. This type of behavior is accepted, and people get away with it. A coworker getting divorced, for instance, might take her anger out on another female coworker. Three years later she might do the same thing, because she got away with it the first time and became popular among her other female coworkers. There's no reason for her to stop.

According to the people I spoke with, nearly every "hater" got off scot-free. Thus, there's no incentive for "haters" to stop. Haters can hate on, haze, bully, harass, make people cry, get them fired, make them quit - and have fun doing all this—with no repercussions. They can take out their anger, resentment, mental issues, and jealousy on the target and get away with it. In some instances, they are even getting rewarded: A promotion, aka the target's old job once she's been forced to resign. So what is the hater's incentive to stop? Why should they stop if they can get away with it? If you knew you could do whatever you wanted and get away with it, why would you stop? In an ideal world the person would have a CONSCIENCE and MORALS and stop, but this obviously isn't the case.

We can't help but wonder WHY this person is doing this to us. What does she want? What is her purpose? Do women do this for kicks? Why aren't they out to get the male species? What motivates them to go after her own kind? What makes somebody behave this way? Why ask— there seems to be no solid answer to this question. Every person and situation is different. The reason one female behaves in a certain way is completely different than another female. Whatever the reason our female coworkers behave the way they do—the point is *they are*.

Ask a hater why and she'll most likely blame her target. After all, whose fault would it be? Certainly not your haters fault! If your hater is behaving a certain way, it's because you deserve it and it's only due to your actions. Haters will always be able to come up with an excuse to rationalize and justify their behavior. Possible reasons to consider are:

She needs to win

Some women are so concerned about getting ahead they won't let anyone stop them and will leave a trail of destruction in their path. To her hating is essential for survival. She'll do whatever it takes to be on top. It's her playing field and she needs you to lose so she can win. She can't afford to be shown up. Winning let's her know she's the best and nobody's better than her.

An event

Did an event trigger her hating? Did something happen at work? Maybe another coworker, not you, got promoted or was chosen for the job she wanted. Doesn't matter that it had nothing to do with you. She is acting out her pent-up rage and frustrations and taking them out on you. Or perhaps something outside of work, that you weren't privy to, triggered it. Think of the myriad of ways we're challenged outside of work. Many haters bring that baggage and drama with them to work, solely to take out their anger and frustration on others.

Revenge

You know that woman who you were competing against for your recent promotion? Just because she's smiling on the outside doesn't mean she's smiling on the inside. Revenge isn't always immediate. It's often a "dish best served cold". Beware: You did something to get on her bad side. Intentional or not, she doesn't care. Point is you're now her next target. There's a reason for the saying, "Hell hath no fury like a woman scorned".

You're doing a good job

Some coworkers may genuinely like you – that is until they see how well you're doing. You might not be bragging about your newfound success, but that doesn't mean your boss isn't. If your supervisor praises you, but not them, they feel insulted and take it personally. Often women, especially the jealous and mean ones, don't want to hear anyone get complimented and raved about. They take it personally and make it all about what they aren't doing. Haters will play the comparison game and will feel threatened when you do well. This in turn makes the claws come out. Women hate other women who succeed, especially when they are trying to succeed themselves.

Bad timing

You're in the wrong place at the wrong time. She had a bad morning – runner in her stocking, her cat threw up, she left her lunch at home (which is incidentally a typical morning for me, but I digress). She's in a bad mood and who is the first person she runs into that morning in the parking lot?

Lucky you! She takes out her anger and frustrations on you. When she sees you do nothing, she continues.

Jealousy

The female world is full of envy. Sometimes women focus on what other women have and hate on them for it. "We often hear that people who feel envious of their coworkers try to bring them down by spreading negative rumors, withholding useful information, or secretly sabotaging their work", says Professor Aquino, who conducted the study with coworkers from the University of Minnesota, Clemson University in South Carolina and Georgia State University, *Science Daily* reports. Maybe she isn't advancing in her own career and is jealous that you are. Maybe she is jealous of you and what you have. Maybe it's your shiny straight white teeth. Maybe it's your alabaster complexion. Perhaps your Ivy League degree or your MBA. Maybe even your hot, dark ethnic fiancée with the foreign accent (which I would love to have BTW). You have something she wants and it's driving her nuts to the point that she's willing to drive *you* nuts in return. In an attempt to even the score she'll try to bring you down.

Seniority

She wants to make you quit. She wants seniority. She wants to show you that she is the best and can outlast anyone.

It's a game

Congratulations- you're her toy. Only this isn't a Jackie Gleason and Richard Pryor movie—this is your life. Some females like to play games and consider you, or anyone else that gets in their way, just another checker on the board that they must get rid of. According to Patricia Spindel, "Some simply enjoy the power they can exert over another, and prefer to play mind games, entertained by watching the negative effects of their actions on others. Their behavior is intended to feed their constant need for stimulation, and it helps to defend against feelings of personal insecurity or boredom."

She wants attention
She is seeking attention and by trashing you she has a captive audience. If your hater is ignored, she'll continue her behavior until it earns her attention.

She's crazy
Does your hater show no remorse? Act in a cold blooded, calculated manner? She's a psychopath. She needs to be on medication or home where she can't hate on anyone.

Biological disorder
Some haters' have a mental or physical disease that causes them to be unaware of or apathetic about their negative behavior. Personality disorders - such as depression, bipolar, and schizophrenia - could also be accountable for your female coworkers' behavior.

Addiction
Maybe she's an alcoholic. Maybe she's a gambler. Maybe she's a pill popper. Maybe it's a prescription or maybe it's something she purchases every night at 4am on the corner of Near Death and Hangover Ave. People can lose the ability

or incentive to judge whether their actions are offensive when they're under the influence of alcohol or drugs — or coming down from them. If she has an addiction and she can't get what she needs while at work she'll take her withdrawal out on you. "Their addictions rule their lives, and unfortunately, when they enter the workplace, the lives of others as well". (Spindel, 2008, p. 41) "Those who abuse drugs or alcohol, or engage in problem eating, gambling, or sex may bring unhealthy interpersonal and family dynamics into the workplace". (Spindel, 2008, p. 41)

Control
It's a matter of control. She wants to control you and she can't. Some people enjoy the power and control they lord over others. They like to watch them squirm and show them who is boss. Maybe she has no control in her own life and is thus seeking it wherever she can.

She's incompetent
Don't assume that all your coworkers are competent and can do the job they have. Maybe she's not competent for her job and needs to get rid of anyone who sees this. Maybe her boss is about to catch on to her and she wants her/him distracted. Best way to cover up her own faults and deficiencies? Shove the spotlight onto you — especially if you're a newbie.

You stood your ground
You stood up to her. You took a stand, probably publicly, against something she wanted. Yes, you were right, which

makes her out to get you all the more. She's shocked that you stood up to her, because most choose not to.

You don't support her
You refuse to go along with her ideas and what she wants. Whenever she suggests something you always have a better idea. She is used to getting her own way and not having to explain and justify her ideas to anyone—especially you.

She's unhappy
Maybe she's not happy with her life, her job, her current position, her finances, or her family. Perhaps she's bored. Maybe she's overqualified for her job or doesn't have enough work to do. Maybe she has no life or hates the one she does have, but more importantly who cares? She has no business taking her unhappiness out on you—but that still won't stop her.

She's difficult to work with
She's evil. She's a horrible person. She's miserable. She's a bitch. She doesn't care. She has no conscience. No morals. No ethics. She is soulless. She is a social deviant. She doesn't know right from wrong and she doesn't care. She's the reincarnation of Hitler. Need I say more?

Her upbringing
Perhaps your hater had a stormy childhood or a bad upbringing. Perhaps that shaped her outlook on the world and her need to lash out at people. Maybe her parents argued a lot or went through a nasty divorce. Her childhood conditioned her to think that hating was acceptable

behavior. A normal way of interacting with people. A normal way of life. Abuse is a cycle for them. It's the only thing they know.

Your current circumstances

Is there something going on in your life that makes you more prone? A hater may be more likely to come after a target when the target is experiencing vulnerability in their life. Maybe you have a husband out of work, a sick child, or you're going through a divorce. Perhaps you're vulnerable, because of a life crisis — the death of a loved one, illness, concerns about your children or parents, or financial difficulties. You spend your time concentrating on your situation and your work, neglecting the underground hating occurring to get you out. Unfortunately, some people can sense when someone is vulnerable or weak and move in for the kill.

Her past experiences

All of which has nothing to do with you. Perhaps she was a hating target herself and she adopted a "strike first" mentality. It's still no excuse.

Au revoir

She's on her way out and wants to take someone down with her. Maybe she wants to show management that she's not the only one with a performance issue. Maybe she wants the company to realize that you're the one that should be on the way out instead.

Work stress
She is taking out her work stress on you. Maybe her department is short staffed. Maybe she's working on a demanding project with a looming deadline. Maybe her boss is verbally abusive to her.

She's the boss
Or at least that's what she thinks and she wants to put you in your place since you're new. She's on a power trip. She's probably been there a while and feels you owe her respect and should treat her as if she's someone important, which in her eyes she is. These haters will openly hate on you—though most likely when a boss is NOT present. For them, the bigger the audience the better—more attention for them.

Work's a competition and you're an unwilling participant
Some professions feed on competition. In female-dominated occupations, such as waitressing, nursing, teaching, it becomes an eat or get eaten environment. Especially when part of the job consists of competing against each other. Which waitress will get the best station? Which realtor will score the listing? Which CSR takes the most phone calls per day? Certain jobs seem to condone, if not promote, this competitive behavior. Whether you knowingly chose to be in it or not, it can lead you right to the unemployment line. Competition is fierce and this makes the claws come out. It's a way of life, but it doesn't have to be down and dirty. Unfortunately, some women just don't like the competition and will do whatever it takes to have you eliminated from the game early on.

You're different than her

And she can't stand it. She can't relate to you, because you're different than her and she doesn't understand you. Hell, she doesn't *want* to understand you. Perhaps your work style differs from hers. Your ethnicity. Your clothes. Your accent. Your education. Maybe you have different beliefs than her. After all, she isn't your Siamese twin, so why shouldn't you? Perhaps they are political. Maybe religious. Or possibly even something as simple as child rearing. Whatever it is, she can't let you stay there. She feels threatened, because you're different or because she has a preconceived notion about your differences.

She no longer has a use for you

Your hater wanted something from you. She got it. You're no longer of any use to her. Don't let the door hit you on the way out.

You're in her territory

Some women view the workplace as their territory. Newcomers beware: If they don't like you or feel threatened by you, don't even bother fixing up your desk- you're as good as gone. A woman who feels like you're a threat will do anything to guard her territory.

Rivalry

Females don't want to work with other women they view as rivals. "You are her rival. She considers you an equal who might at some point knock her down a notch. You might get the promotion or the man that she's after". (DiMarco, 2005, p. 21).

She doesn't like you

She just doesn't like you. There's no logic. No rhyme no reason. For whatever reason she just doesn't like you — your appearance (height, hair, skin, figure), age, weight, sexual orientation, marital status, recent engagement, youth/age, material possessions, your office is bigger, you're more attractive, you dress better, you have a graduate degree, the boss likes you more - whatever the case may be.

You're a threat to her

Is she threatened by you? Your title? The quality of your work? Your education? Some women feel threatened even if you work under them or don't even have the required degree to take their job. The easiest thing to do to someone who threatens you? Get rid of 'em.

She wants to hold you back

She has a desire to keep people down and hold them back. Thus, she doesn't want to see you get ahead or succeed. She has issues with other women getting ahead and will try to hold you back on the job in hopes you quit.

Low self-esteem

Perhaps she's suffering from low self-esteem and "needs" someone to hate on to feel better about herself. Maybe she feels like she's an insecure nobody, so it makes her feel better to make you feel like one too. She'll feel better if this powerful/attractive/youthful/or wealthy person is derailed off-track and brought down to her level. None of this is your fault. You're an unfortunate target. She's most likely done this before. Perhaps to the person who was in your position prior to you. Hell, maybe that's why the previous person in your position left. Guess what? Eventually you'll leave too. It shouldn't have to be this way, yet it is.

Your work environment

Some work environments are more conducive to hating than others. Is leadership weak? Is there little or no teamwork? High employee turnover? Is management often absent or not available? Some internal factors that influence hating are leadership style, working conditions, lack of communication, heavy workload, restructuring of organizations, layoffs, lack of support, and most importantly, an environment where there's no intervention for the target. According to Beswick, Gore, and Palferman, 2006, "Whether or not bullies are able to target individuals in organizations often has more to do with the organizational culture than with a target's characteristics. Role ambiguity or role conflict, and weak or inadequate organizational leadership, along with a lack of control and a generally negative work environment can lay the groundwork for the bullies to begin jockeying for position."

Management doesn't care

Does management encourage hating by looking the other way? Do they refuse to acknowledge it? Do they laugh it off when it's reported to them? Many organizations just don't care or are in denial. They prefer to do nothing but wait and hope it will blow over. However, by doing nothing they are condoning the hating and allowing it to continue. Incidentally, this isn't a company you want to work for. Some companies are more concerned with the bottom line.

For instance, the restaurant I worked at made money, so they didn't care if their employees were hating on other employees. Plus, several of the waitresses had been there for over ten, some even over twenty-five years. The owners put their personal friendship with their staff ahead of their employees' well-being. The staff knew it and used it to their advantage.

Your position
Some might have a position at work that makes them more vulnerable or makes them stand out. In this case, it's not about the individual, but their position.

An oops!
A past disagreement? A miscommunication? A misunderstanding? A conflict? Did you somehow unintentionally offend her in the past? You may not even realize you upset her. She doesn't care if you know or not. She doesn't fight fair.

It's fun
Some haters enjoy hating on others so much they do it for the fun of it. It's like an addiction — they can't stop. And why should they? It's done at the expense of others. They get their kicks out of seeing other people squirm or even lose their job. To them it's pure entertainment. Would you like a soda with that popcorn? Once again, it's not you- it's your hater. I know that's not much consolation when you're in the unemployment line for the third time in a year and all your friends and family are questioning your work ethics.

She's full of anger and hate

She needs an outlet; congrats, you're it. She could be full of hate for many reasons, relating to or not relating to work (bad marriage, in-law issues, sick parent, addiction). But I can almost guarantee you, the reason she is full of hate has nothing to do with you. She just wants to take her anger out on an innocent target. Her train of thought: I'm out to get you. I'm going to sabotage you and harass you. I'm going to make you so miserable until you quit. Oh, and btw, don't take it personally.

To discipline you

It's just discipline to her. She has a parent-child view of you. She feels like she needs to assume the role of disciplinarian and scold you to put you in your place.

No reason

Maybe she has no objective. She's just a mean girl.

She thinks she's better than you

Some women just feel that they are superior and better than others, which is how they justify their behavior.

Because she can

Why not? The real reason hasn't changed. Going back to my initial sentence- they are doing this **BECAUSE THEY CAN!**

Melinda

Melinda, 24, had just started a customer service job. The work was pleasant enough, as were her coworkers. She was happy, until one day when she was in the bathroom stall at work. While she was in there, three of her female coworkers came in and started gossiping about her. They talked about everything, from her work, which they called "sloppy", to her clothes, to her high-pitched giggle. "And the worst is that she's clueless and genuinely thinks the people here like her", one said as they laughed, walking out the door. Melinda was in tears. As she cleaned her tears she wondered: Had they done this before? Had they talked about her to other people? Were other people talking about her? Melinda became extremely paranoid. If someone looked at her funny or sounded off, she imagined this person was talking about her too. She became increasingly withdrawn at work. She stopped talking to her coworkers for fear of giving them something else to talk about. Gradually, her performance began to suffer. She never confronted her haters or let on to anyone what she'd overheard. She eventually quit her job with nothing lined up for fear of being eventually fired.

Unfortunately, Melinda's story isn't uncommon.

Joanne

I connected with Joanne on Facebook. She told me, "If they want to get you out they will do whatever it takes." So true. She was terminated after only one year as a police woman. One of the deputies took an instant dislike to her, thus the hating began. She was blackballed and made to feel unwelcome. Joanne felt isolated and shunned. No one talked to her. The few that had been friendly to her outside of work in the beginning, unfriended her on Facebook. Meanwhile, she was under the radar (her words). Everything she said or didn't say would be taken out of context and she would be written up. As it was still during her probationary period, she wasn't eligible to be part of the union so they did nothing to help her. She was terminated and filed a lawsuit. It went to court, but the judge dismissed the case.

She changed careers after that. Her next position was at an insurance company. She was always treated differently, but never complained. She rarely asked for time off and when she did, she would be denied. Yet everyone else got days off. She eventually complained to Human Resources. She questioned why she couldn't leave early or get time off. Human Resources went to her manager, which of course made things worse. Her manager yelled at her for going to HR, in front of the whole office, which gave her a panic attack.

The hating persisted. Unknown to her, several coworkers were spreading rumors about her. One of the rumors was that she was harassing another employee. The rumors got back to HR and her manager. She was reprimanded, even though there was no proof. An emotional basket case by then, she went out on FMLA, which her company denied. They made her go for an evaluation for a second opinion. Upon returning to work, she found out that two coworkers <u>hadn't</u> said anything; that in fact it was the coworker she was allegedly harassing that had started the rumors. Apparently, she was jealous because Joanne had gotten the job she had applied for—that explained what this woman had against her. Unfortunately, her company had now labelled her as a troublemaker and was out to get rid of her. Unbeknownst to her, while she had been out on FMLA, HR had suspended her for a lapse in her insurance license. What lapse? They fired her the first week back for failure to renew it and follow up on the "certified" paperwork they had sent to her home— "certified" paperwork that to this day she has still never received. She was terminated, even though HR later verbally admitted to her that they had made a mistake. She is currently pursuing legal recourse. Her legal situation was still pending when we last spoke.

"It's a pretty basic technique. You use people's vulnerabilities against them. Sometimes you just have to play dirty."
Jane,
-Jane the Virgin

Why Always Me?

Does your female coworker leave you wondering why she hates you so much? Has this happened to you more than once? More than twice? Numerous times? So many times that you've begun to doubt yourself? Your sanity? Are you left wondering what you did to deserve such punishment? Why does she hate on you as opposed to the person next to you? Is there something about your character, history, background, or attitude that makes you more apt to be hated on? Why do women keep hating on you specifically? Why not your Mom, sister, cousin, or coworker? Have your friends and family come to doubt you? Do you wonder what you're doing wrong? Have you come to expect it when you start a new job? Have the people with whom you interact (friends, family, partner) also come to expect it? Does the thought of meeting your new female coworkers grip you with fear? Do you find yourself asking these questions? The good news is it's not you and you're not alone. The bad news is that it might be something you do subconsciously.

Many people spend a lot of time, strength, and energy trying to answer the questions- *Why me? Why always me? Why does this keep happening to me*? Because it can happen to anyone. Haters do not discriminate. "Individuals can be victimized no matter who they are, how old, devoted, loyal, creative, experienced, organized, responsible, how much initiative they demonstrate, or how much a team player they are" (Davenport, Schuartz, and Elliot, 2002, p. 71). It's unfortunate, but hating can happen to the most intelligent, educated, creative, attractive, and successful people.

You weren't a bitch. You didn't provoke it. You weren't out to get anyone. You didn't go to work and refuse to do your job. You didn't act up. You didn't shirk your duties or responsibilities. You suddenly didn't become incompetent, inept, uneducated, or unemployable. You're not underperforming. You're not unqualified for your job. You're contributing to the company. You're meeting your goals. Yet, you're the one being hated on. And maybe it's not the first time.

"What did I do?" is a common reaction and self-doubt. You're not crazy. There is nothing wrong with you. Don't doubt yourself—that's what she's banking on. She wants you to feel ashamed and embarrassed. Even though you don't deserve to be hated on, there's something about you—your behavior, your position, your appearance—that gets your hater worked up and brings out her desire to turn on you. Something about you set off her evil bitch and the hating started.

It's hard not to take it personally when your female coworker is hating on you. How could you not? However most of the time it has nothing to do with you, so don't bother thinking too hard wondering what you might have done to offend her. Maybe you got the job she wanted. Maybe you remind her of a former friend. Maybe you enjoy work and she doesn't. Maybe she hates all blondes. Maybe your education makes her scared. Maybe she is just plain mean and nasty and you have the misfortune to work with her. None of these circumstances have anything to do with you. It's all her—her past, her preconceived notions, and her way of dealing with things. Chances are you're not the only one she's done this to.

What people (your friends, family, and coworkers) need to understand is that you didn't ask for this. Your hater selected you as her target. "Ironically, and sadly, the victims are portrayed as the ones at fault, as the ones who brought about their own downfalls". (Noa, Disler Schwartz, and Pursell Elliott, 1999, p. 20). You didn't wake up one morning and tell your female coworker to defame you and ruin your good name. You didn't invite her to humiliate or ridicule you. You did nothing to warrant her behavior. You didn't ask to be mistreated. You didn't choose to be her target. You didn't ask to be harassed. You didn't ask to be hated on. You didn't ask to be subjected to your female coworker's daily bashing. How you're being treated isn't fair and not your fault. You were singled out and hated on. Your hater chose you — you do not deserve to be hated on. No one would bring all this on themselves; they'd have to be a masochist. Ignore the people who don't understand- they are clearly clueless and ignorant. They're lucky it's never happened to them. Unfortunately, being hated on makes you stand out. Your fault or not, you now have a black X on your forehead.

The subconscious ways you may scream target

You may be asking yourself *is there something wrong with me? Am I doing something wrong?* Or more importantly, *am I doing anything right?* Unfortunately, some women may take your success personally and equate it with their failing. Haters often select targets who are highly competent, accomplished, popular, or high performers. This poses a threat to your hater, whom always wants to be viewed as the best. Adams (Oct 11, 2006) stated that "...contrary to common perception, targets of workplace bullies aren't the underachievers, the slackers, and the deadwood. Often they're very capable and productive employees whose competence threatens the bully." FYI- **Someone else's success has nothing to do with their failure.**

Perhaps she thinks you're less likely to tell and more likely to leave ASAP. Haters tend to go after those they see as weak. Unfortunately, shyness, quietness, and being a people pleaser (just to name a few traits) are often mistaken as a lack of confidence and haters go after those that are less likely to stand up for themselves. By saying nothing, you invite them to continue their behavior. Stand up for yourself – they've chosen you because they didn't think you would.

Haters go after "nice" people. "Bullies interpret "nice" as the unlikelihood of being confronted or stopped." (Namie and Namie, 2009, p. 58). Some view being a nice person as a character flaw and weakness just waiting to be exploited. Haters target "nice" women in hopes that they will be least likely to fight back, report, confront, or question what is happening to them. Haters love nice people, because nice people will continue to be nice, even after the hating has started.

Has something about you made you more prone to attack? Can you ever be held responsible? Is it ever our fault? Do we ever bring any of it on ourselves? Do we portray ourselves as an easy target? Do you have a vulnerability or weakness that she is aware of? Do you tell your coworkers too much- things they can later use against you? Do you bond and let your guard down with your female coworker too quick? Do you lack self-confidence?

Are you an introvert? If you constantly and consistently do some of these things you could be contributing to your situation.

- You're a people pleaser.
- You're strong.
- You're smart.
- You're empathetic.
- You're a good listener.
- You're compassionate.
- You're independent.
- You pay attention to what's going on around you.
- You avoid standing up for yourself.
- You're attractive.
- You're intelligent.
- You're her rival—she considers you her equal and fears you may someday go after something she wants or has.
- You're competent.
- You're highly skilled.
- You're accomplished—according to Susan Shapiro-Barash, highly accomplished women are more likely to be the targets of woman on woman aggression.
- You're dedicated.
- You're passionate.
- You're well-liked.
- You're shy.
- You're respected.
- You're unassertive.
- You're devoted.
- You're loyal.

- You're organized.
- You know what you need to do. You get it done. You don't need to ask for help.
- You speak your mind.
- You're ambitious. (Bet you never thought you'd hear that being ambitious might hurt you.)
- You have aspirations and goals.
- You do a better job than she does.
- You're trusting.
- You're naïve.
- You're a good networker.
- You're successful.
- You're imaginative.
- You have a sense of humor.
- You're helpful.
- You're honest.
- You possess integrity.
- You say what's wrong.
- You say what's right.
- You offer suggestions on how to improve things based on your past experiences (perhaps the changes would affect your hater).
- You ask a lot of questions. You question people and things.
- You voice your opinions.
- You're a team player.
- You're an overachiever. She wants to be the best. She can't have you going above and beyond. Therefore, she needs you gone.
- You're educated.

- You're talented.
- You're good at what you do.
- You have good manners.
- You're well spoken.
- You love your job.
- You're good with people.
- You're confident.
- You're charming.
- You're younger than she is.
- Bad luck. Why not? It certainly isn't good luck.

Most importantly: Why always you? Because you're better than your hater and SHE CAN'T STAND IT!

Victoria

I'd known Victoria for almost ten years. She called me one day, extremely excited, to tell me about the new waitressing job she had gotten. She'd been laid off and was struggling to make ends meet on unemployment. Naturally, I was happy for her. She showed up to work on her first day and eagerly started trailing another waitress, Sarah. She would be trailing Sarah for the first week and then getting her permanent schedule. She soon realized that Sarah was more than what she had bargained for. She wasn't the only one following Sarah, another new employee- a woman named Helen- was also trailing her. She quickly realized that Sarah's strategy was to turn new waitstaff against the owner and each other. Sarah started making derogatory statements to them about every single person working at the restaurant. She told them that she was quitting her job, because she hated working for the owner. She said that he constantly yelled at her for other employees' mistakes and that he had a "volatile disposition", which had caused several others to quit.

Victoria remained silent. She listened quietly, but with worry. What if this was true? The owner seemed so nice and she really needed this job. It was close to her house and the hours worked perfectly with her daycare provider. Sarah continued with her comments. She told them that the owner hated the restaurant industry and was going to "close up shop soon". Victoria started to wonder if maybe she should look for another job.

Whenever Helen was on break, Sarah would say hateful things about her to Victoria. She'd complained that she shouldn't have to train two people at once and that she didn't think Helen would be able to "pull her own weight there". Soon, Victoria noticed Helen giving her strange looks. She feared that Sarah was saying negative things about her to Helen.

After completing her tumultuous training with Sarah, Victoria called to find out her work schedule. The owner was short with her and told her he would call her after the lunch rush. He never did. Victoria called a few days later, only to be told that she wasn't on the schedule for the next two weeks. Victoria went in the following week to find out about her schedule. The owner took her aside and said, in a matter-of-fact tone, that he wouldn't be hiring her. He told her that Sarah had explained to him that she just didn't "get it". Mind you Victoria had been waitressing off and on for over twenty years. Victoria, deeply dismayed, ran out of the restaurant in tears after trying to explain to the owner what Sarah was doing. She opted to send him a certified letter detailing Sarah's behavior, to which he never responded.

Madeleine

I connected with Madeleine on Facebook. Madeleine was a victim of mobbing by some mean girls who never grew up (her words). She told me that she believes that haters choose their target because they perceive them as a threat or they take the weakest from the pack and go in for the kill. Madeleine had been at a jeweler's for ten years, but was at a vulnerable place in her life when the hating started. She had recently lost her father and her mother was undergoing treatment for breast cancer. She had just come back from FMLA. She had never been written up for job performance. In fact, six months prior she had been named employee of the month. She wondered if that wasn't part of the reason the hating started. Upon returning, her team started to have a lot of closed door meetings which excluded her. When questioned, they would claim it wasn't necessary for her to be in the meeting. She noticed lots of whispering in the cubicles near her. She could tell that her desk had been riffled through. Paperwork she needed would suddenly go missing. She would be reprimanded. She was eventually terminated for her "inability to perform her job". Of course, there was nothing to back this up. Fortunately, she was able to collect unemployment and get severance pay. She, like most other targets, was relieved to be away from the mobbing. Madeleine had last heard from a former coworker that her haters had started in on someone else right after she had left, and her new target was in a quandary over what to do. She also heard that her missing paperwork surfaced in one of her hater's office.

Unfortunately, her next position had a hater too. Her hater had been there over ten years and had seniority, which she took advantage of. Madeleine was off site a lot and would get hated on over the phone where there were no witnesses. Fortunately, she documented it via email to her counselor and Facebook messages to friends. Her hater would criticize her for minor things — nothing she ever did was right. If she called a client, then she would be yelled at for not emailing them. If she emailed them then she was chastised for not calling them. Each time she tried to quit, her boss always promised the work environment would improve. Staff turnover was 90% while she was there, due to the hard time and negativity her hater gave everyone. Most people declined to do exit interviews and quit without notice. Several even walked off mid-shift in tears. She almost quit several times and finally did, per the advice of her counselor. She left her boss a letter and her key. She belongs to a Facebook support group for survivors of narcissistic abuse. She is happy she left on her own terms (power) even though they denied her unemployment — which she heard they always did. She fought them on the denial of her unemployment claim, citing that she left for health reasons and prevailed. She was still looking for work when we spoke

"They can be charming, presentable, socially skilled, professionally successful and well-regarded by superiors. They can also be workplace bullies."
–Dana Wilkie, Editor at Society for Human Resource Management (SHRM)

160

What to do? What to do?

What do you do when your female coworker has set out to destroy you? There's no right or wrong answer — there are multiple ways to handle this situation. What might drive one employee to quit- might make another employee confront someone- while another employee might ignore the situation altogether. How you deal with your hater depends on your background, your self-esteem, your self-confidence, your ability to get a new job, your finances, and your courage — in addition to extrinsic factors, like your hater and your company.

In many ways, what to do is linked with why she's chosen you. If we know why, which we usually don't, we know how to react. When I found out why my mentor had encouraged another Spanish teacher to blackball me, I could have changed my behavior and altered my teaching style. I could have stopped doing French Club. I could have stopped doing French Honor Society. I could have stopped doing the popular after-school pizza fundraiser. I could have stopped my interactive communicative teaching methods. I could have gone in and taught more conservatively (blandly) and tried to blend in by not getting involved, not doing anything out of the ordinary, not going above and beyond what was required of me. I could have given boring lectures and handouts to my students. No one would have felt threatened. But why should I have had to do any of that? Why should I have to change my personality and teaching style? Shouldn't the students come first? If they are happy, motivated, learning, and there are no parents complaining, then shouldn't I have been left alone?

Personally, if I had to do it all over again I wouldn't go quietly. I'd confront the teachers who were hating on me and lawyer up.

Unfortunately, most targets wait a long time before doing anything. Some hesitate because they think that the situation is their fault and they must have said or done something to bring this on themselves. Some targets fear that others will blame them, especially if it's happened to them before. Others may feel ashamed or think that no one will care. Some are afraid that reporting the hating will make things worse, and thus delay in reporting it. DON'T LET THIS BE YOU. You probably aren't the first person your female coworker has hated on. Chances are, you probably won't be her last.

Some targets never come forward. When you do nothing, your hater views that as a welcome sign to continue her hating. "The target may also delay action, hoping that with the passage of time the bully will stop. Unfortunately, the bully interprets all inaction as submission." (Namie and Namie, 2009, p. 54). The situation isn't going away on its own, which means you need to come forward. By staying silent and doing nothing, you risk being her doormat because she'll most likely continue her behavior. Look at it this way — a kid steals a candy bar and no one catches her. She does it again. Maybe no one sees her or maybe no one cares, because it's just one candy bar. So, she starts to do it every day. Then twice a day. Why not? There's no reason or incentive for her to stop.

Address the situation as quickly as possible. The longer it continues, the more damage it will do to your career. Decide in advance what you're going to do. If you do something rash in the heat of the moment, you may regret it later. If you plan to wait until the next attack, decide what you'll say and don't let the heat of the moment derail you. **REMEMBER**: If violence, threats, harassment, or something else extreme is involved, going directly to your supervisor and Human Resources is your only choice.

Individuals respond differently to emotionally upsetting circumstances. Some may pick up a bad habit to help them cope. Any type of vice (smoking, overeating, shopping, prescription meds) you use to get you through the workday may be helping you psychologically, but the problem isn't solved. Some people may even react physically. *Do not* become physically violent at the workplace. That's the last thing you need. If you feel like you're going to snap you need to *leave immediately*, whether that means going home "sick" for the day, going out on FMLA, or quitting *without* giving two weeks' notice. Doesn't matter how it looks to others or what they think. They will think worse of you if you get taken away in handcuffs.

Wouldn't it be great if all you had to do was stand up for yourself and the hating stopped? In the ideal workplace, outing your hater would get her fired. In the ideal workplace, if you treated people with dignity and respect they would treat you the same way. As the world isn't fair, don't expect the workplace to be either. The question is: What is the next step? Do you want to continue to face ongoing humiliation, day after day? Or do you want to attempt to thwart her in her path? What can you do that doesn't risk retaliation or more abuse? Is your goal to get her fired, get her transferred, or just to get her to leave you alone? Besides quitting, confronting her, or ignoring it, is there another solution? **NOTE: Sitting around and feeling sorry for yourself isn't an option here!** React when the hating starts; don't react when your termination papers are being typed up. REACT WHEN YOU FEEL SOMETHING IS OFF.

<u>Report it</u>: Don't assume that management and Human Resources know what's going on. If everyone made that assumption it would never get reported. Plus, the more times your hater gets reported the more susceptible they become to a future lawsuit and the more apt your company is to do something about it. Describe what has happened as clearly as possible. Be exact. Give examples. State the facts, not opinions. Management doesn't care how you feel (sorry!) — they care about the facts. Don't call her crazy, a psychopath, or anything else, even if she is. Hopefully, they'll be smart enough to figure out what kind of person she is. **Tip**: If you're not her only target you might want to consider reporting her as a group. This might prompt management to take it more seriously and they won't be able to blame you.

- **<u>Go to your boss</u>:** The first conversation you have should be with your boss. How good is your rapport with her/him? If he is a male, would he understand or tell you that you're being paranoid? Will it affect your working relationship with her/him in the future? Your yearly review? If it happened again would you feel comfortable going to her/him a second time? Is the hater also one of her/his direct reports? This might be more challenging if your hater reports to your boss, especially if they are on great terms and have known each other longer. If you decide to meet with your boss, document it. Even if the response is favorable you don't know what will happen in the future. In the Human Resources world, one way we document things is to send an email to ourselves. That way you have the time and date stamp on it. After all, if it's not documented it never happened.

- **Go to Human Resources:** That's what they are there for. Any reputable employment law attorney (if it gets to that) will ask you what role Human Resources played in resolving the issue. If you say you never reported it to Human Resources, it lessens your chances in court. If everyone appears to be working well together and there are no complaints, then they probably aren't looking for any signs to the contrary. They might not know something is wrong unless you tell them. There could be severe repercussions for the hater. Some unforeseeable, because unless you're also in Human Resources, you don't know what else she has in her employee file. You never know, she could have a bad performance review and they may be looking for reasons to fire her. This could be the icing on the cake. At the least if you come forward Human Resources can't "pretend" they didn't know. Not that Human Resources would EVER do that! If you don't report your hater, there's no way your situation will improve. Please note that even if you do report her, there's still no guarantee management will help you. Remember Human Resources **does** work for the company. In addition, if management doesn't properly resolve the hating, it could get worse.

Ignore her: Ignore her hating and hope for the best? Hope she gives her two weeks' notice tomorrow and moves across the country? Hope she's in a car accident and dies? Don't react to her rude behavior. Don't look at her when she makes a comment. She may be seeking attention — don't give it to her. Maybe (but probably not) she'll stop when she sees that you're ignoring her. Don't let her bother you. Appear indifferent. Act like you don't have a care in the world. Be strong.

Wait: But for what? For her to stop? For you to be transferred? What are you waiting for? If you're actively interviewing for jobs elsewhere then maybe you want to consider waiting her out and doing nothing. Maybe creating stress in a short-term situation isn't worth it. Maybe now isn't the time to act. Maybe it's better to wait and observe. Is she hating on others too? Use this time to compile a dossier on her and observe how she treats others. Bide your time. Your hater will eventually put herself in a compromising position if she continues and that is when you can go in for the kill.

Prove her wrong: Make your professional reputation such that nobody would possibly believe her hating. Make your coworkers want to question her thoughts and the truthfulness of them. Unfortunately, your coworkers need to have an open mind for this to work.

Befriend her: Is it possible to convert your hater into an ally? Would you even want to? Is it something you even want to try? Would you ever be able to trust this person? Show her you want to be her ally. Let her know that you respect her, her work, and aren't out to get her or her job.

Common ground: Find common ground. Do you have anything in common with your hater? Anything you could try to bond with her over? A shared interest? Hobby? Group? If so, how can you leverage this to your advantage?

Kill her with kindness: I've tried this before and it doesn't usually work, but you can try it nonetheless. Ignore what's going on and just smile and go about your work. I think this fails, because your hater ends up thinking you're clueless and just carries on. But maybe your kindness will make her feel guilty and she'll stop her hating and stay away from you.

Flattery will get you everywhere: Sometimes a hater is just looking for a little attention. So why not give it to her? Compliment her, whether it's work-related or not. I know it's the last thing you want to do, but by complimenting and making a fuss over her you're building up her self-esteem. In addition, you're making her happy and who better for her to shower her happiness on than the person standing in front of her making her happy- you! Make a fuss over her. Yes, I'm serious — it may make you want to vomit, but it could work. Will it make her feel bad for mistreating you? Maybe. Will it humanize you in her eyes? Possibly. Let her think that you admire her, look up to her, and think she has something you don't. You may be surprised at the results. If she continues she'll look bad, especially since you were so nice to her.

Retaliate and fight back (most don't recommend this): Did you ever get angry with a friend, family member, or ex? Did you ever want to get even? I know I have! Go after her. Avenge yourself. What's fair is fair. Fight back. Hate her right back. Whatever she does, do it back. She gossips about you; you gossip about her. She "forgets" to give you a phone message; you "forget" to include her in a group meeting. Behave in a way that will dissuade your hater, and future ones, from going after you. Pro: Once she sees you mean business she may stop her hating. Con: Her hating may increase tenfold. **Warning:** Your actions reflect on you, not her. Remember, you want your actions to disprove the attacks being made on your character. It doesn't matter what she said, did, didn't say, didn't do—if you're caught and disciplined that will all be water under the bridge. You'll be held accountable for **your** actions. So, if you choose this route, proceed with caution. You may want to get even, but that doesn't mean you should. However, it doesn't mean you shouldn't either. If you feel you may eventually quit or be fired, why not go out in style?

Get her fired: Play dirty. Be aggressive. Beat her to the punch. She's got a weak spot. We all do. Whether she comes to work late, makes a mistake, forgets to do something—find out what it is and use it against her. Copy her boss on important emails that make it look like she's not doing her work. Set things up to get her fired.

Micromanage her. Do things she should be doing before telling her or before she can get to them. Then tell her you did them. This will make her feel inferior, inadequate, slow, and useless. Change her calendar or her bosses' calendar in Outlook to make her look bad. Create schedule conflicts and then call her on them. Find a way to get rid of her- observe her enough and she'll give you a reason.

Ask for a transfer: A transfer to a different department within the company isn't always possible, but has worked for some. It never hurts to ask.

Find a mediator: Find a coworker who is a mutual "friend" with you both. Get some advice from her on how to handle your hater. Does your hater have a hating pattern? If so, how have her past targets handled her? If her answer is, "they quit", then a red light should be going off. Why did they quit? Was it reported to management? What was their response? Was Human Resources involved? Would she be open to sitting down with the two of you? Let a third party, someone who has nothing to lose or gain by the outcome, act as a mediator. The negative side of this? This person could end up turning against you with your hater's influence or they could become your hater's next target, for which you'll undoubtedly be blamed.

Safety in numbers: If your hater has another target you've found an ally. Bond together to fight back. There's strength in numbers. The more people that complain, the more likely management will believe you.

Manage the way people perceive you: Perception is everything. Try to frame yourself in the best light possible. Influence how you want your coworkers to see you, not how the gossipers and backstabbers in your office have portrayed you. Is this fair? No. Should you have to do this? No. But picture yourself as your own BFF and your female coworkers as your own worst enemies. The latter are out to get you and sabotage you for no reason. Be your own PR person. Market yourself the way you want to be seen.

Work-related conversations only: Tell her via email, so you have proof, that you only wish to have work-related conversations with her AND that you don't want her discussing non-work-related things about you with others. You have the legal right to have a work only relationship only with her.

Reframe your way of thinking: Change your thoughts and feelings. Or at least shift your perceptions to the point that you're comfortable enough to stay there. Reframing is a tool used to change the way you look at something. Although "reframing" won't change things, it may help you cope better with your current situation. Yes, I know that's weird. Yes, you're entitled to your thoughts and feelings. I'm not saying they are wrong—they are completely justified. But what if your thoughts are doing you more harm than good?

Stand up for yourself: If you don't, who will? DO SOMETHING! Let your hater know that her behavior is *not* okay. It's not acceptable. Hold her accountable for her actions. You're your own best advocate and ally. Show people that you're not a victim, an easy target, or a scapegoat. Speak up right away. Don't let it continue. Don't let your hater think she can get away with it. "Unfortunately even the most capable employees hesitate to speak up about their treatment. Namie (2003:3) has reported that targets of workplace bullying endure their pain, on average, for 22 months. Unwilling to react to aggression with aggression, many targets choose to keep their torment hidden until they can no longer bear it. Even though most targets are bright, capable people, the wearing effect of constant bullying can undermine even her self-confidence. When people ask why targets don't speak up for themselves, they are asking from the privileged position of someone who has never been targeted." (Spindel, 2008, p. 68).

Let others know who you really are: If you know she's spreading rumors about you to others, talk to the coworkers hearing the rumors. Set them straight if you know what the rumor is. Unfortunately, it's your word against hers. If they are friendly with your hater outside of work or have worked together for a long time, they probably won't care or will take her word over yours.

Call a truce: Attempt to make amends with her. Okay, you haven't done anything wrong, but tell her you want to start fresh with her. Tell her that perhaps you somehow got off on the wrong foot and want to start anew.

Avoid her: Is it someone who you can avoid? Is it even possible? Or would she go out of her way to find you?

Unfortunately, this can be time-consuming and stressful. But then again so is looking for a new job.

Email her: Many are opposed to this and for good reason- which I discuss later. Emails can live forever in today's technology, and emails on your employee email account are company property. From the Human Resources perspective, yes, you can get into trouble for doing something non-work- related at work, like sending a personal email. If your emails are monitored and you were to get into trouble, they might ask you why you didn't go to Human Resources. The pros of sending an email? You have time to organize your thoughts. You get out what you want to say without being interrupted. It's also less confrontational. Less she said/she said. Remember in person, she's more apt to deny your accusations. With email there's a 50/50 chance she'll respond. Cons? She can forward it to everyone you know and alter the text in it. Worse yet, she can reply, add her friends to it, and write you back attacking you even more, denying your accusations, and making you look bad.

Career coach: This isn't a psychologist. A career coach specializes in job issues. A career coach can be a good sounding board. Whether it's performance, policies, or dealing with your female coworker, it can be useful to consult with one. You can discuss your situation with one and take the stress off of your friends and family. You can get advice on anything from leaving your present employer, to updating your resume, to applying for jobs, or even help on staying where you are. She/he can help you pick up the pieces if you lose your job. She/he can help you redevelop your professional identity (how you see yourself) and your brand (how you market yourself). She/he can also help you set new career goals.

Play dumb: Note use of the word *play*. Acting nice and playing stupid is confronting the situation in a non-confrontational way. This can work if your hater has been friendly to you in the past and you have established a work relationship. Mallory, 35, did exactly that. She attempted to "talk" to her coworker, Darcy, about some rumors she had heard. Mallory said, "You'll never believe what Georgianne in accounting told me. She said you've been telling everyone that my divorce is my fault. Don't worry—I didn't believe a word of it *and* I defended you." This makes you seem nice and chances are Darcy will feel bad (if possible) and find someone new to hate on.

ADA: An individual with a disability is defined by the American Disability Act as a person who has a physical or mental impairment that substantially limits one or more major life activities, a person who has a history or record of such an impairment, or a person who is perceived by others as having such an impairment. After all, isn't her hating impairing you mentally? Ask for a reasonable accommodation up to and including a transfer. I personally don't know anyone who has tried this and don't guarantee it will work, but anything is worth a try at this point.

FMLA (Family Medical Leave Act): Provides temporary relief from the situation. Hating can bring on serious health conditions that can make you unable to perform the essential functions of a job. FMLA is one of the best pro employee laws out there. It was the first bill President Clinton signed in 1993. (Bush Sr. vetoed it in 1990 and again in 1992). However, not everyone is eligible for FMLA. Your company MUST have at least 50 employees within a 75-mile radius. In addition, you must have worked there for at least twelve months or 1,250 hours over the past twelve months. Request your FMLA in writing, preferably by company email. Don't forget to BCC your home email. If your company denies your leave or tries to get you to delay or postpone it, I'd be wary as they might have plans to fire you first. It may be the time to consult an attorney. Upon returning from FMLA you must be reinstated to your position or a similar one. Showing that you went out on FMLA due to hating can help your court case. This shows that the hating had you so anguished and mentally incapacitated that you were unable to function and perform your day-to-day work activities. You can use this time to decide what to do, update your resume, and even apply for jobs. Remember, even though it IS illegal for employers to retaliate against someone for using FMLA, that doesn't mean it's not done. If they attempt to demote you or force you to quit, you need to consult a lawyer, because this is illegal. Potential damages for a FMLA violation can include reinstatement, front and back pay, and liquidated damages. If management is aware, but doesn't care about your hating situation, be prepared when you go back. Management may up the ante to get rid of you if they've decided to choose your hater over you. In addition, who knows what she's been doing behind your back while you've been out. FMLA can delay the inevitable and buy you time. I had a friend go out on FMLA due to female hating. She flew down to a spa in Mexico where she spent three weeks resting, relaxing, destressing, and recharging. To this day she says it was one of the best decisions she ever made. She said if she hadn't she would have eventually said or done something to get herself fired. She was able to come back in a better mental state to deal with what awaited her. Even though she was far from happy, it enabled her to spend two more years at her job. When her division relocated she got a handsome severance package and was able to collect unemployment. I understand we don't all have the resources to use FMLA to "get away" as most people have commitments that would prevent them from doing so. However, just getting away from the office should be a vacation enough in itself. (NOTE: FMLA is NOT intended for a vacation and you could be terminated for abusing it if your company were to find out.)

Go public (like I'm doing now): Hold your company accountable for what they've allowed to occur there. When all internal grievance procedures have been exhausted tell your story. Go to your local newspaper or TV station; blog online, do whatever you can to show the world what kind of place you work at — and the kind of abuse they let happen.

Seek legal representation: Talk to a lawyer and explore your legal options. See if you have a case. This can be done whether you decide to stay or go. It may cost a lot of money to speak to a lawyer, but it will cost even more money if you lose your job and health insurance. If possible, find a lawyer who will take your case on a contingency fee basis—which means he won't get money unless you do.

Lastly: Remember if you're ever physically threatened, please report this directly to the police.

DON'T...

- Act defensive. If you act defensive people might wonder if the allegations, rumors, and stories are true. They'll wonder what you're trying to hide.
- Let her destroy you. Anger and bitterness will ruin you.
- Let her occupy your life outside of work. I know it's hard not to think about the torture inflicted on you that day and fear what awaits you tomorrow at the office. But you need time mentally away from her (which is why people don't live at their jobs). Don't allow her to take over your brain. She doesn't deserve to take up any more emotional energy and space in your head than she already has.
- Let her influence the way you think about yourself.
- Let your emotions control you. Don't let your feelings dictate your actions. Yes, I know women rely on them for guidance. Put them aside.
- Try to change her. You can't. Don't waste your time and energy even thinking about ways to make her change. If you have that much spare time you should be updating your resume (just in case!).
- Take her behavior personally. It's all about her. She is the one with the problem—not you. She's probably done this many times before and gotten away with it. Because

of that she continues to behave and treat her female coworkers this way.

- Spend your free-time thinking "what if?" You'll drive yourself crazy. What if I win the lottery and never return to work? What if she dies tomorrow? What if I'd never taken this job? You get the point? Forget the "what ifs" — it is what it is.

- Try to control her. You can't. The only person you can control is you. You can only control your actions and how you react to your female coworkers' hating.

- Be in denial. You didn't want or ask for this hating, but it's happening. You need to figure out your next plan of action and how you'll deal with it.

How you respond to hating shapes and defines who you are and how you perceive yourself. Become a force to be reckoned with by finding a creative solution. Watch: Most people won't try to undermine you a second time. No matter what the outcome is, you're better than your hater. Know this and hold your head up high. Remember it's about her. She's acting out, based on whatever reasons or preconceived notions she has.

If you see someone being hated on, stand up for them. You never know — it could be you next time. No one is immune from being the target of hating.

Kesslyn

I connected with Kesslyn on LinkedIn. She had recently gone back to school to complete her MBA, while working a full-time job. As she was newly divorced and raising two kids alone, she opted to spend her lunch hour studying to free up her evenings for her children. Because she turned down lunches with her colleagues to study, her "friendly coworkers" translated this as her bragging and her being too good for them. Her former lunch group started telling everyone that Kesslyn was telling people that she was too good for her current position. They planted other stories too. They became rude and interrupted her while she was completing training on a new marketing phase. Kesslyn could see other coworkers, and even her boss, start to distance themselves from her. Kesslyn was eventually let go without a valid explanation or a paper trail to back up her dismissal. The standard "not a good fit" phrase was what her boss gave her. Kesslyn got her karma because as she told me, "They were all eventually fired too, because the true colors of their craziness were revealed".

Mugette

I connected with Mugette on Facebook. Her story was one of the more heartbreaking ones I would come to hear. She had been out on disability for the last eight months and would most likely be on permanent SSI by the publication of this book. She had endured hating while working at an insurance company for almost five years before she finally spoke up. She was at the breaking point by then and would panic at the mere thought of going to work.

The hating started almost immediately. Her haters would complain if she took an extra three minutes for lunch or count her trips to the bathroom. She received notes left in her locker telling her to wash her clothes better and calling her a slut. She gave the letters to her manager and was told they would do something about it. All management did was blame it on someone who had quit. She'd see her coworkers whisper about her and laugh. One even went so far as to slam a door in her face. Another one pushed her out of her chair. The office was very competitive and 90% female, both of which she believed caused the hating. She was also a very accomplished professional. She'd been working in the insurance industry for over 20 years.

Human Resources was of no help. They only told her to document things. One HR representative even went so far as to tell her to go to the doctor and get a "happy pill". Feeling hopeless, she called the 1800 number her company had listed for complaints in the employee handbook. It was allegedly an anonymous number (note use of the word *allegedly*). Apparently, the anonymous hotline for employee complaints wasn't anonymous (gee, imagine that). Someone found out and told everyone. Everyone stopped speaking to her. Her boss joined in on the mobbing. Her boss refused her breaks and would follow her to the bathroom and stand outside, while loudly berating her for spending too much time in there. Mugette sent an email to HR documenting this. Around the same time, she had a breakdown and couldn't leave the house. Human Resources told her to go on disability or return to work. She returned to work and Human Resources said they never told her to return. HR took away her badge and keys and fired her. She filed a claim with the EEOC that was still pending when I last spoke to her.

"We smile at our enemies while scheming behind their backs devising ways to even the score."
-Anonymous

Confronting Her- or Not!

To confront or not- that is all too often the question. Most women don't know what to do when they find themselves as another female's target. *Should I confront? How will it look to others? Is it worth it? Will it create a hostile environment? Will I lose my job over it? How dare she — who the hell does she think she is, anyway?* Choose your battles (or not) wisely. Do you only want to confront her because she made you mad? Do you want to make her look bad in front of others? What do you want to gain from confronting her? What is your goal?

Most people don't start a job with an action plan in place on how to confront a coworker. Unless, of course, they work at Intel. According to a 2009 article from CBS News, Intel provides all new full-time employees with "constructive confrontation" training, which teaches people to attack the problem, not people, and to do it in a positive manner. Employees are taught how to confront a coworker who is abusive to them. Their goal is to not let the bully win and not to have their good employees leave.

It's not easy to keep quiet and you shouldn't have to. I once resisted saying something to a coworker who had spread rumors about me. I didn't lose my job over it, but it was annoying nonetheless. Months later I ran into her in a department store- I figured this was God's way of telling me to go for it — and I did. She clearly wanted to be a bitch to me, but because I presented my thoughts in a clear, concise, and friendly manner, she couldn't pull out her claws without being the bad person. It was obvious she wasn't used to being confronted and being held accountable for her actions. Naturally she denied everything. Did she really think I'd believe her denial? Hell, she didn't even have the guts to admit to what she'd done. She played the victim card and claimed she didn't know what I was talking about. Unfortunately, this is a common reaction to expect when confronting someone. After all, they usually operate behind our backs and don't have the guts to do it to our face. Luckily, I got the chance to confront her after regretfully not having the opportunity to do so while in the same workplace. Go me!

Confronting her

If her hating is causing you instability on the job and damage to your professional reputation, then how can you not confront her? If I had confronted my haters, I'd probably still be at Sayreville. Sure, the drama might have escalated, but that might have forced management to intervene.

Most people choose not to confront, which is most likely what your hater is banking on. Haters like it when people don't stand up for themselves. When targets choose to do nothing but suffer in silence, this enables the hater to persist in her hating activities. "Further, the longer a confrontation with the source of your pain at work is postponed, the less likely that action will ever be taken to stop the bully". (Namie and Namie, 2009, p. 69). Your female coworker needs to know that her hating isn't acceptable. Let her know you have no problem calling her on her behavior. If you don't confront her, she'll continue her hating. People treat you the way you allow them to.

When we settle for unacceptable behavior, we encourage it to continue.

By fighting back *immediately* and confronting your hater, you let your hater know that you'll speak up and won't look the other way. Your chances of success go up when you confront your hater after the first or second incident. By saying nothing you are giving her permission to hate away. Who knows—she may even stop once she realizes you'll stand up for yourself. But don't expect her to ever like you.

In the 2014 CareerBuilder survey nearly half (48%) of workers who were bullied at work took matters into their own hands and confronted the bully in an attempt to discourage it from happening again. Of these workers, 45% stated they were successful in stopping the bullying while 44% said it made no difference and 11% said the situation worsened. A 2013 study conducted by the Workplace Bullying Institute found that 68.8% of targets confronted the bully, and in 93% of cases, the bullying didn't stop. Don't let these findings deter you. However, even if you confront your hater don't expect her to stop the hating forever. At best, she'll stop hating on you. You're only one person—you alone won't be able to change her behavior.

Hating can turn the calmest person into an emotional basket case. Wait until your anger has subsided before confronting her, even if this means waiting until the next day. If you confront her in the heat of the moment, you risk letting your emotions guide you. You don't want to end up yelling at her or crying in front of her. Flying off the handle won't help your cause, especially if other coworkers overhear you, and particularly if your hater has painted you as an emotionally unstable person. The last thing you want to do is have a meltdown and give credence to her tales. Choose a moment when you're calm. A day when you have time. Perhaps a day when your boss is out of the office or you have less work than usual. You may also be shaken up and need time afterward to compose yourself. I recommend confronting her at the end of the day, so if it doesn't go well you'll be that much closer to leaving.

A one-on-one confrontation is preferable as it's better not to have an audience. She may see bystanders as a personal attack and increase her hating tenfold if she thinks you want to make her look bad in front of others. If more than one person is involved, you must decide whether to confront them together or individually.

NEVER NEVER NEVER put your grievance to her in writing, especially via company email during work time. The only exception to this rule, which, as you may recall, I've done, is sending a letter on your last day on the job. Chances are you'll never see your hater again and assuming it's non-threatening, you risk little to nothing. That being said, it could still wind up in your Human Resources folder there. Writing a letter is tempting, especially for women who like to avoid direct conflict. However, writing can leave the interpretation wide open. Not to mention, if you email her, she can forward it to everyone and complain that you're harassing her. Unfortunately, you have now put something in writing that she can take to her boss or even worse to Human Resources. Don't forget, every email you send can be considered Exhibit A in the courtroom.

Tell her you have some concerns you would like to discuss. Choose your words carefully- remember everything you say can and will come back to haunt you. Politely and firmly tell her you'd like her behavior to stop. Be as specific as possible with names, dates, and times. Give examples. Tell her, "I don't appreciate it when you _____" or, "It has come to my attention that rumors about me are being spread around the office and that the information originated from you. I would appreciate it if you come directly to me if there's something about me that you feel merits addressing." Lay down your boundaries and tell her what you expect from her from now on. For example, "If I make a mistake please tell me and not the whole office."

Stay focused on the situation, and don't let her bring up past issues, as they're irrelevant. It doesn't matter that you accidentally threw out her lunch from the refrigerator two weeks ago. You're there to confront her on *her* behavior. By all means mention something you agree on or make a positive comment, so long as it is relevant to the discussion at hand. For instance, "I wanted to speak with you regarding my arriving late last week. I was disturbed to hear you told everyone. I think it's great that you're so time conscientious and the team appreciates your punctuality, but..."

Don't be surprised by her response. Don't expect her to be ashamed, embarrassed, or guilty. If anything she may be angry or annoyed; after all you're wasting her time. She may feign shock and innocence. After all, she has no idea what you're talking about (sarcasm). If she did do something it wasn't intentional. Most likely, she'll be nonchalant. After all, she doesn't care as she hasn't done anything. Nothing is wrong (yeah right!). She's your ally and would never do anything to hurt you. By getting it all out in the open you are letting her know you're watching her. Even if she plays Miss Innocent and denies her wrongdoing, she now knows that she'll have to watch her back more carefully in the future.

If all else fails, give it to her straight. For instance, "I have no intention of quitting my job. I need to make a living. You're not going to run me out of here. Cut the garbage. We're professionals. If you have a problem see a counselor, the boss, or Human Resources, but don't bring it into the workplace." You can even go as far as to tell her that if she doesn't stop, you'll report her to management or Human Resources.

Explain to her the negative impact her hating is having on her career (even if it's not true). You never know, one day it just might be. If you frame it as being in her own self-interest she'll be more apt to tame her hating ways.

End the confrontation peacefully. You aren't there to argue; you just want her to stop. If you're unable to rectify the situation, you may have to end the conversation. Keep the mood professional and offer to see the boss together. Tell her, "I don't think we're going to reach a solution. Let's discuss this with a manager." This shows you're cooperative and looking for a resolution, not out for revenge. Don't be surprised, though, if she refuses.

When confronting your hater, REMEMBER:
- Be serious.
- Remain professional.
- Stay calm.
- Act tough. Let her know she doesn't scare you. You aren't threatened.

- Look her in the eye. Even if she looks away, do not avert your gaze.
- Don't waiver.
- Stand your ground.
- Keep your emotions in check. Detach yourself from the conversation, if necessary.
- Get straight to the point. Do not pause. Get everything out before you allow her to speak.
- Use her name. Using someone's name is a form of assertiveness. The most beautiful sound to someone's ears is the sound of their own name. Stroke their ego.
- Rehearse it in your head beforehand, or with a trusted friend.
- Confront her without malice.
- Keep your arms at your sides. Crossing them or putting them on your hips may be construed as confrontational.
- Exude confidence.

When confronting your hater, remember DON'T...
- Expect her to agree about what has occurred.
- Stoop down to her level.
- Call her names (even though you want to. Save it for the car ride home).
- Let her push your buttons.
- Antagonize her.
- Beg or plead for her to stop.
- Threaten her.
- Yell.
- Have an attitude.
- Put her down.

- Give her anything to use against you.
- Become too emotional. **Crying and yelling are not allowed.**
- Allow her to make you back down.
- Make any personal blows. (It's okay- I know you want to!☺)
- Let her rationalize and explain away her actions. Don't accept her excuses. Hold her accountable for her behavior.
- Use sarcasm.
- Whine.
- Waste time with chit-chat, stories, or humor.
- Attack her — doing that will only put her on the defensive.
- Make a scene.
- Tell her how you feel. She doesn't care. If she did she wouldn't be behaving this way and you would not be having this conversation.
- Agitate her. You don't want things to escalate.
- Beat around the bush.
- Suggest reasons for her behavior.
- Let her manipulate you.
- Let her change the subject (she may try).
- Act angry.
- Be defensive.
- React. She wants to set you off and make you look bad. She wants to make you so upset that you make a scene. She wants to portray you in a way that makes you look unbalanced or crazy to show that her actions were justified. If you have a meltdown everyone will agree

with her — you need to be gone! Remain cool and your credibility will surface in the end.

Document that you confronted your hater and that you told her that her behavior was unacceptable. I recommend sending an email ASAP from your work email to your personal email. You then have a time-stamped document that you have access to outside of work. If you confront her and she doesn't stop, then confront her again. Call her on her hating. Tell her you already asked her once to stop. Make it clear you want her to leave you alone.

Let your hater know that you mean business and you're not going to let her walk all over you — you're not a doormat. Inform her that you have little to lose by confronting your hater. What do you risk losing — your "wonderful" job?

Reasons not to confront her

The thought of confronting a coworker that you see every day, maybe even multiple times a day, might not be at the top of your to-do list. In fact, taking a stand against a coworker can ruin your career and fast-track you to the unemployment line. You must ask yourself: *Is she vindictive? Has she been with the company for a long time? Exactly what will it cost me (both in the monetary and non-monetary sense)? Does she know people in high places? Is it worth it?* If you decide to confront her, keep in mind several factors- she might have peer or managerial support, you might get fired, or the hating might intensify.

The Human Resources professional in me wants to remind you of a few things- work is for work-related conversations only. This might turn out to be more than that. Just be careful it doesn't get too nasty. Some people, who have confronted a coworker, have had the coworker claim they are harassing them. The last thing you want is someone filing a harassment complaint against you. Your hater is obviously someone you can't trust and we already know she is capable of mudslinging and hitting below the belt.

Many people choose not to confront their hater for a variety of reasons:

She has connections- If your hater is BFFs with someone in top management, updating your resume and packing your bags may be your only option. Once your hater has turned upper management against you, there's little you can do, short of taking legal action.

Not worth it- Your hater won't just drain you of your energy, but also waste your time. Some feel it's just not worth it to confront their hater. They ignore her and look the other way. They don't care, have better things to worry about, or don't want to waste their time and energy on the hater gossiping about them. If it's something minor, maybe it's not worth the confrontation. For instance, Keisha's coworker told everyone that Keisha arrived ten to fifteen minutes late to work every day. Was she? Yes. Is this any of her business? NO. Is she Keisha's boss? NO. Is she Keisha's Human Resources Manager? NO. Keisha had more important things to do, like please her boss, than worry about her coworker's big mouth.

Don't want to make things worse- Confronting her can help, but it can also have the opposite effect and greatly worsen the situation. By standing up to your hater, you risk being humiliated and further attacked by her. She may be mad and take her anger out on you. Things can always escalate and get worse than what they currently are.

Temper- Sometimes people with a temper will look the other way. Why? They know how they are and they know they risk a big blowup if they say anything to their hater. Even if they're in the right, they feel that a confrontation would be too big of a risk and keeping their job is what's most important—not their coworker's tales. It can be difficult to confront someone and have a positive outcome. Emotions take over, tempers flare, and next thing you know angry words get said in the heat of the moment that can't be taken back. If her hating has no impact on your job, then it might not be worth it to confront her.

High blood pressure or other health issues- If you have high blood pressure and are told to avoid stressful situations, you may choose to do your best to ignore your hater.

Your source is questionable- If what you heard isn't coming from a reliable source, you might want to avoid a confrontation. Make sure you have all the facts straight before you risk making an ass of yourself.

Human Resources- If your hater works in Human Resources she should be ashamed of herself, because Human

Resources represents the company. They are the police, so to speak. They monitor and enforce rules and settle employee disputes. If your hater is discussing confidential information in your file you must go directly to her boss-ASAP. This is extremely unprofessional and should not be tolerated.

Hilary

Hilary was super psyched to start her first job out of college. She was even happier when two girls her age took her under her wing her first day there. The three would eat lunch together and talk about their lives outside of work. Hilary noticed how they treated Sue, another coworker of theirs. Sue had been there just under a year. Her friends wouldn't even say "hello" to Sue or respond when Sue said hello to them. They'd merely say mean things about Sue, while Hilary sat in silence. Her new pals eventually noticed that she was not chiming in on the Sue-bashing. When questioned, Hilary told them that she didn't even know Sue and that Sue had never done anything to her or given her a reason to say anything bad about her. From that point on, Hilary could feel her two friends slipping away — coffee breaks taken without her, texts never returned, and work-related projects that excluded her. While Hilary never actually heard them bash her, she was quite sure they were. They certainly had no qualms bashing Sue.

One day her boss requested a meeting. Hilary was shocked at the reason why. Her boss said that two of her coworkers (her former friends) had come forward and complained about her. They alleged that she was lazy, didn't meet deadlines, procrastinated, delegated her work to others, and came in late. As Hilary had been there less than 90 days, she was fired on the spot. When she tried to justify why her coworkers would say these things and mentioned the "Sue bashing dynamics", her boss said that he didn't want to hear it. He had made the decision and did not appreciate her questioning his judgment and calling two seasoned employees liars. Hilary packed up her desk. She went home and put in her unemployment claim. Fortunately, it went through undisputed.

Cassie

Cassie was 42 when her boss retired and more than ready to be promoted to Senior Director of Compensation and Benefits. Cassie had over 20 years of Human Resources experience, a BS in psychology, a MS in HR, and an MBA. She belonged to numerous committees and had chaired several of them. However, Cassie found out she was up for the promotion against her coworker, Betty. Betty wasn't as qualified, experienced, or educated as Cassie. The last time she had been up for a promotion against Betty, vicious rumors had circulated (leaked by Betty and her friends) that Cassie had only gotten the promotion due to her "friendship" with the Vice-President of Human Resources. Between the stares and whispers Cassie had been in tears every day. The last straw had been when a friend of one of her coworkers came up to her at the food store to tell her she'd heard about her affair and asked if she was getting a divorce—all asked within hearing distance of Cassie's family.

Cassie had no interest in going through all this again. Betty's lies and slander had taken all the joy out of her promotion. Why risk it all again? Going through that once was more than enough for Cassie. But, in the end Cassie went for it. Her husband and family encouraged her. Unfortunately, Betty still had it in for her. Cassie received the promotion easily, no questions asked. But she received the silent treatment from her new team. They treated her with disdain, on the rare occasions they spoke to her. They were difficult to manage and didn't help with her transition. She finally sat down with her team and questioned them. A new team member came clean. She said that Betty had been spreading rumors about Cassie, which she didn't feel comfortable repeating. Cassie went straight to Betty, who didn't deny it and told her that she wasn't going to stop— and she didn't. Cassie continued to have difficulties with her team. People became less friendly and gradually stopped responding when she greeted them.

Cassie opted to quit. She was so sick of Betty by this point; she had ruined her two promotions and made work miserable. She didn't bother speaking to management. If she ever saw Betty again it would be too soon. Luckily, she lined up a new job within a month, with a larger salary to boot.

"You can kill a person only once, but when you humiliate him, you kill him many times over."

-"The Talmud"

Should I Stay or Should I Go?

The good news is that you're in charge of what you do. Obviously, that's not the case with a termination. However, no one is forcing you to stay. If, and when, you leave is up to you. Unless, of course, you have a spouse who has some input on what you do. There will be negative consequences involved no matter what you do, but recognize the positive potential of both outcomes as well.

I can't tell you whether you should stay or go. Only you can decide what kind of environment you want to work in; there's no right or wrong answer here. Each hating issue is different. Each situation is unique and each individual makes their choice based on things going on in their life. Each person is different. What one person might be able to tolerate might drive another to suicide. In the end the decision is yours—unless your job makes it for you.

As you weigh your options, consider the following questions: Can your family and health survive if you try to stick it out? Will things change if you stay? Will management eventually stop your hater? Do you really want to leave, and if so, do you want to leave quietly? Would you rather leave on your terms or wait until someone makes the decision for you? Would you regret your decision to resign if she decides to leave soon after?

In most cases the goal of your hater is to get you to leave. Most often, hating leads to the target's voluntary resignation or termination. "Targets of bullying often are forced out of their positions—either because they are fired, encouraged to leave, or they simply can't take it any longer" (Barnes p. 84). I didn't have to make the decision to stay or go at Sayreville; my employer made the decision for me. I knew I would be fired, so I opted to wait for that so I could collect unemployment, as opposed to resigning to save face. As I didn't have the financial resources to go without an income, unemployment was my best option. As unhappy as I'd become, if I hadn't been terminated I would have returned for a third year there, as I had no savings or spouse to fall back on. Many targets of hating have no choice, financially, but to stick it out until they are fired so they can collect unemployment.

I've heard many times that females have an easier time finding a job—even if that's true, they certainly don't have an easier time keeping it. I've never met anyone who made up their mind to keep their job and succeeded in doing so. That doesn't mean you can't. It could happen. But then again, free healthcare and a free higher education system in the United States could also happen someday too.

Most of the targets I encountered chose to quit their jobs rather than confront their hater or report her to Human Resources. Most people find this the easiest and least stressful option. However, if you leave quietly, *your hater wins*. Moreover, why should you have to leave? Do you really want that? Some may decide to stay; after all, if you quit your hater gets exactly what she wants. My advice? Don't let her win.

You have three choices- quit, wait for your company to fire you, or stay and try to resolve the issue. Whether you stay or go, you'll need to deal with the side effects. Figure out the lesser of the three evils and determine what you can live with in the end, as well as what you can handle financially. There will be consequences if you stay and consequences if you leave. Let's explore the options of leaving your job and trying to keep your job, along with the side effects for both.

Staying

Wanting to leave and being able to leave are very different things. For most people, earning a living isn't a luxury, it's essential. Unless you're wealthy, you most likely need to work. When the unemployment rate is high, you may be willing to stay and tolerate things you wouldn't normally. You may be financially trapped and have no choice but to stay and endure the hating. Unfortunately, both your hater and your employer know this. In a bad economy, targets are more likely to stay at their job, which only prolongs the abuse. Leaving your job in a bad economy could put you out of work for years to come and you could end up losing everything—your car, your apartment, and so forth. Meanwhile, your hater stays employed and zooms in on her next target.

Some might want to leave, but can't. Perhaps there's no demand for your field. Maybe you're looking for a new job, but can't find one. Just remember that no situation is permanent. It may seem like you'll be dealing with your hater for the rest of your life, but that's not the case. Remember: All three of my main haters left Sayreville within a few years after getting rid of me.

People may stay out of fear of the unknown. They don't want to get a job and experience the same thing or worse. Women who have already experienced hating and switched jobs before are also more likely to stay. It's scary, but lots of women will tolerate hating for fear of how others will view them if they switch jobs yet again. While I've never stayed at a job where I was experiencing hating, I've stayed at jobs where I was not appreciated, and was underpaid and under-employed, because I was not harassed by female workers and feared the alternative. I was comfortable where I was and didn't want to tempt fate.

Others may find themselves staying for various other reasons. Sometimes a job search can come at an inopportune time. Let's say you plan on moving, but you're not sure where. It would be better to be sure where you're moving before you end up with a hellacious commute. In a situation like this you may need to put off your job search. Not necessarily because you want to, but because you have to. Older workers may fight to stay, not because they want to, but because they fear ageism and difficulty finding a new job. More experienced employees who may not be able to find anything close to their current salary also opt to stay.

I once worked with a woman who was being bullied, but was forced to stay, because if she left on her own within a five-year period she would be forced to reimburse the company for the classes she'd taken for her MBA.

Coping mechanisms

So you've made up your mind to stay. Good for you. Whatever your reasons are, it won't be easy. You'll need tremendous mental strength to get through it. If you're going to stay and stick it out you'll need to develop coping mechanisms for your own sanity or you'll have no choice, but to leave for your mental health.

Please yourself: Do little things to make yourself happy. Give yourself some TLC. Go out of your way to see friends and do things that you enjoy. Concentrate on the things that make you happy, smile, or laugh. Keep busy outside of work, so you don't have time to dwell on what your hater has inflicted on you today or worry about what she'll do to you tomorrow. Work out at the gym. Join a club. Take a class. Get a pedicure. Do something you've always wanted to do like sky diving.

Find an outlet: If you really, really, really must stay and you absolutely have no choice (most likely for financial reasons) find some ways to destress yourself. Take up kickboxing or karate- envision her face. Things that have helped me include- the gym, facials, and massages.

Professional counselor/therapist: You may think that <u>you</u> don't need to see a therapist—your hater does. I agree. However, she's currently put you in such a mental state it might be beneficial for you to get it all out and vent to a professional. Someone you don't know, who can offer you unbiased advice. Please seriously consider consulting with a therapist on an ongoing basis.

Give yourself a daily mantra to recite: Anything to boost yourself. Look into the mirror and love yourself. Tell yourself how great and fabulous you are. You are intelligent, smart, accomplished, and considerate. You are you and your hater can never take that away from you no matter how hard she tries.

Get a support system: Surround yourself with friends and family that will listen to you and offer you their love and support during this trying time. (Note: If a friend tells you that they need a hiatus, they were never really your friend.)

Think positive: The power of positive thinking. Be grateful for what you have. Stay hopeful. Make a list of reasons to be happy. At least you don't live with this person. She's not your family.

Focus on the future: Make a list of where you want to be in five years. Doing this will allow you to visualize your future without her. Know that all situations are temporary and do not last. My Mom always says, "This too shall pass". I guess that's one way to look at things when your female colleagues go after you. You don't have to spend the rest of your life working with her. She's just someone you have to temporarily endure. It's not permanent. Look at today's volatile job market- layoffs, hirings, and firings. Hope for the best — maybe her husband or partner will get a transfer and she'll leave. Maybe you'll get a promotion and be done with her. Of course, I know all of that is easier said than done.

Eat well: It's all about healthy choices. Nutrition. Don't overindulge. I follow a healthy vegan diet, which I highly recommend. Keep yourself healthy.

Laugh: Laughter is the best medicine. Find the humor in things. Get your positive endorphins up and flowing.

Meditation: Rest and relaxation. Practice breathing. Try yoga. Find your inner peace and beauty. Namaste.

Vent: Venting always helps. This is easier nowadays with all the social networks readily available online. I use my Facebook status to bitch and complain. That way I can hear from other people who are or who have gone through something similar. It helps to blow off steam. Don't keep it bottled up inside you. Get it out. Find a group or better yet — start one.

Pray: If you aren't religious now is a good time to start. I'm not telling you to pray that she gets hit by a bus or finds another target. Pray for the strength and courage to stand up to her and do what needs to be done. Pray for the strength to understand your situation. Pray for a solution. Pray to be able to get up every morning, go to work, and face what awaits you. Pray to find the power to do what you need to do to end this situation (I don't mean to kill her as much as you may want to). Read the Bible. Seek religion. Talk to a pastor or minster.

Side effects on targets who stay

Every person is unique. How one person reacts to hating is different than another. Each person has had a different set of life experiences which has brought them to this point in their life. Some people may be able to brush their hater's actions and words off more easily than another. Some may find it so debilitating that they are unable to get out of bed in the morning without quitting or going on prescription meds.

Hating has many side effects. The side effects each person experiences are not necessarily the same. Some may develop depression or other mental health problems as a result of constant attacks or attempts to bring them down. "The constant replay of perceived persecution, futile attempts to escape, and revictimization can wear some targets down to the point where they become depressed and contemplate suicide. This is one of the things that makes psychological harassment so dangerous. No one knows what another person's personal history has been. When predators attack, even they may be unaware of the degree to which they set off an internal chain reaction in their targets by triggering original feelings of unworthiness or unbearable pain. It is these internal reactions that can lead to sometimes devastating consequences." (Spindel, 2008, p. 66).

If you decide to stay and stick it out, for whatever reason, prepare yourself for the mental anguish that awaits you. While emotional abuse isn't visible, its impact can be just as devastating and long-term as physical abuse might be. "Because employees' economic livelihoods or pensions depend upon staying in their jobs, they may suffer irreparable harm, or exhibit post-traumatic stress symptoms. This is a very high price to pay to earn a living." (Spindel, 2008, p. 37)

Hating won't just affect you or your job. It will affect those you love and those around you. It will spew over into other relationships — family, friends, and other colleagues. Staying will impact your outlook on life, your mental health, and your physical health. Depending on what outlet you find to take your emotions out on, it can affect your finances too. It may affect you when you cook. Your mind concentrates on your hater. You burn yourself. It may affect you when you drive. Your mind concentrates on your hater. You don't focus on driving and the next thing you know you've hit someone. It's hard to concentrate on anything else when you're driving home daily in tears. I once accidentally tapped a pedestrian—I had just left my teaching job and I was in tears. You get the picture?

The impact hating has on your mental health

- affects parenting abilities
- affects your professional identity, which is very important to some people
- anger
- anxiety
- apathy
- depression
- emotional instability
- grief
- guilt over possibly doing something to cause the hating
- guilt over taking the job
- fear
- feeling abused
- feeling alone
- feeling beat down
- feeling bitter
- feeling defenseless
- feeling degraded
- feeling destroyed
- feeling disempowered
- feeling humiliated

- feeling incompetent
- feeling inferior
- feeling like a coward
- feeling like a victim
- feeling like an outsider
- feeling a loss of control
- feeling violated
- feeling exposed
- feeling weak
- feeling worthless
- feelings of confusion
- feelings of abandonment
- feelings of aggression
- feelings of despair
- feelings of desperation
- feelings of discomfort
- feelings of disgrace
- feelings of distress
- time wasted over worrying and talking about it
- unhappiness
- wounded pride
- feelings of distrust
- feelings of guilt over staying
- feelings of helplessness
- feelings of hopelessness
- feelings of hurt
- feelings of inadequacy
- feelings of rage
- feelings of rejection
- feelings of revenge

- frustration
- feelings of stupidity
- feelings of unworthiness
- moping around
- more prone to having an accident
- irritability
- it kills a part of who you are
- impaired ability to make decisions
- lashing out at others (either at home or at work)
- mentally draining
- mood swings
- reduced quality of home and family life
- restlessness
- self-doubt
- shame of being duped
- marital issues
- loss of confidence
- loss of energy
- loss of friendships — but keep in mind that your friends aren't really your friends if they walk away in your time of need
- loss of morale — not only for the target, but those who witnessed it
- lack of motivation (at work or at home)
- loss of self-esteem
- loss of trust in others
- suicide or suicidal ideations
- not wanting to leave your home
- going on antidepressants

- homicide (which I'm honestly surprised doesn't happen more often)
- hospitalization due to mental issues

The impact hating has on your workplace productivity

- diminished productivity
- absenteeism from work
- failure to reach potential in the organization
- withdrawal from the workplace
- social isolation from coworkers who don't want to be seen with you (happened to me at my teaching job)
- job dissatisfaction
- loss of credibility
- missed work time for doctors' appointments
- loss of reputation
- loss of workplace friendships

The impact hating has on your health

- auto-immune system disorders; i.e. rheumatoid arthritis, multiple sclerosis, thyroid diseases- Graves' and Hashimotos
- digestive problems; i.e. ulcers, indigestion, heartburn, gut inflammation, food sensitivities.
- chronic fatigue syndrome
- adrenal fatigue
- dizziness or fainting spells
- fatigue
- hair loss
- increased risk of heart attack or stroke, which could cause death
- insomnia

- headaches or migraines
- heart palpitations
- flashbacks
- shortness of breath
- skin conditions
- high blood pressure
- loss of appetite
- memory loss
- PTSD
- musculoskeletal disorders
- nervous breakdown
- nightmares
- overeating
- panic attacks
- paranoia
- poor concentration
- substance abuse- smoking, drinking, drugs (prescription and illegal ones)

If you have several of these side effects, you might want to ask yourself what you're doing. Is staying really worth it? Why would you even want to consider it?

Even if you decide to stay you may want to update your resume and start doing networking outside of your job. You never know—just because you've decided to stay doesn't mean they don't plan on firing you next week!

Termination

Most companies think it's easier to fire someone, usually the target, than deal with the situation, which could continue and progressively become worse over time. It's easier to pretend *the target* is the issue and fire her than to punish the hater and open up a can of she said/she said worms. Thus, the organization chooses to blame the target and portray her as the "troublemaker", "not good for the organization", "not a team player", or "causes problems". They think that by firing the target they are getting rid of the problem. Instead this only lets the hater continue on her path to a new target.

Being terminated can cause significant psychological harm to someone. "The toll taken by arbitrary firings is staggering. The financial losses suffered by employees are only the beginning. Psychologists have found that being fired is the second most traumatic experience a person can have next to losing a loved one. The humiliation and self-doubt that people feel when they are fired, combined with the stress of worrying about how they will take care of themselves and their families, drive many people to mental illness, alcoholism, and even suicide." (Maltby, 2009, p. 63). Losing a job, for most, can be devastating. Perhaps it may not bother some people; maybe they hated their jobs and are happy to have a six-month unemployment vacation. Perhaps they were looking for an excuse to retire and the haters gave them one. To others it might be the worst thing that could ever happen to them. "In a matter of a few months, it is possible that a vibrant, healthy competent employee can be driven to ruin- economic, physical, and emotional." (Namie and Namie, 2009, p. 38)

Most companies today don't care about their employees. They'll fire you in the blink of an eye. They'll fire you without warning. They don't care what happens to you and your family. They don't care if you lose your home.

They don't even care if you attempt suicide. In an age where gun violence runs rampant (no thanks to the Republican Party), I'm surprised more employees don't come to work on shooting sprees. And honestly, who could blame the target of such hating?

Good-bye

Who wants to go to a workplace where they are laughed at or humiliated every day? Only a masochist! It's hard enough to get ahead as it is, but vicious coworkers are enough to make anyone have a nervous breakdown. How can you possibly work when you constantly have to be on your toes ready to defend yourself? Who wants to spend their workday trying to avoid a female coworker? Who wants to spend all day preparing a response for the next time they see their hater? Who wants to live like that? Not to mention the toll it takes on your physical and mental health.

When people are setting you up to fail, the writing is on the wall—why would you even consider staying? Do you really want to stay somewhere you're not wanted? Do you want to stay somewhere where you'll be constantly forced to prove yourself to management? Do you want to stay at a job where you are in constant fear of losing it? Do you really want to work at a place where snide remarks, manipulating, deviousness, and other forms of hating are the norm? If you stay, what does that get you: A steady paycheck? More grief and aggravation? Is it worth it? Wouldn't you rather go somewhere where you can be appreciated and not hated on? No one is giving out medals for toughing it out. You shouldn't have to leave your job because of your hater, however, working somewhere where you constantly have to be on your toes can be a great source of emotional and mental stress.

Sometimes the only solution is departure. When nothing changes, it's no surprise that most targets start looking for a new job. Dealing on a daily basis with a hater and management that doesn't care can be incredibly draining. If you've confronted her, complained, and nothing has improved, then quit. It's not worth your time and effort to fight a losing battle. You need to cut your losses and know when to move on. The sooner you leave the less likely you are to be scarred by the hating. Go somewhere where you can be appreciated. Don't feel you need to stay out of a sense of duty, honor, or pride. You need to do what's best for you. Your company obviously isn't looking out for you and most likely, staying won't change that.

In a good economy there may be little incentive to stay. Once targeted, most feel that there's no other way out and the only choice they have is to leave. The unknown and unemployment are less fearful than the known; aka what awaits you at the workplace each day. You come first. Forget about sticking it out if you feel like you'll lose a part of your soul. There's no job that's worth the loss of your sanity, self-respect, and dignity. "Employees who face and witness constant bullying do leave their jobs at higher rates than in civilized places." (Sutton, 2010, p. 125). Researchers Charlotte Kayner and Loraleigh Keashly estimate that 25% of targets leave their jobs. Are we really surprised? Who wants to work in an environment where they are constantly hated on? Why would you want to continue working in an environment that's physically and mentally detrimental to your health?

Leaving before your health and career are affected is a good move. Don't underestimate the consequences for your health, both physically and mentally. Targets of workplace hating have an increase in health problems, whether an aggravation of a pre-existing condition or a new one, especially over an extended period of time. Many targets, even those pursuing the legal route, resign in order to mentally survive.

Not only will your hater make your life at work miserable, but hating will affect your life outside of work too. As most women mentally take their work home with them, they will take the hating home with them too. You'll find yourself spending your evenings replaying what happened in your mind and wondering what you could have done differently. You'll spend your time out of work brooding over it and dreading returning to work. You'll think about your hater while you're driving to work. You'll think about her backstabbing while putting your kids to bed at night. You'll think about her gossip while you prepare your family's dinner. You'll find yourself at your kid's birthday party pondering how your coworker could have announced something mean about you to everyone in the lunchroom. It will preoccupy your time outside of work and you'll find you have less attention for your family. Even when you're physically with your family, you're not mentally there. Your hater is now first in your life, your family a distant second. I couldn't imagine being married or having kids and having to go through what I did at

Sayreville. The experience itself was so draining. What would I have had left over to give my family?

Your hater will not only cost you your job and your health, but also your family and friends too. Friends and family that have never experienced hating may not understand and question your role in the dispute. Even those that do understand may tire of listening to your situation. As a target of hating you could potentially not just lose your job, but also your spouse, family, and friends.

Start looking for a new job ASAP. Experts say it's easier to find a new job while you're still employed. I once interviewed a gentleman who was unemployed. When I asked him why he'd left his last employer he told me that he wanted to look for a new job, but felt it was disloyal and dishonest to continue working there while looking for a new job. I hired the candidate, but not for that reason. Please DO NOT do what he did. Once I got to know him he confessed to the mountains of debt he had incurred and how he deeply regretted his action. DON'T LET THIS BE YOU.

Targets who feel they have no choice but to quit may be denied unemployment benefits. However, if you can prove constructive discharge you may still be able to collect benefits (NOTE: I don't know anyone personally who has tried this, so I can't say how easy or hard this might be). I know that in some states unemployment claims "generally" are less investigated than others. New Jersey is one of the easiest states to put a claim through. Maryland is not. Upon proving constructive discharge, plaintiffs are eligible for all the damages they would be eligible for had they been fired. Constructive discharge is defined as working conditions that have become so unbearable that a reasonable person would be forced to quit.

If management asks you to resign be careful what you put in writing. "Quitting" a job, in most cases and in most states, will disqualify you from unemployment. Proceed with caution if you're asked to sign a release, as you'll most likely be signing away your rights to sue. If you really want to sign it or they pressure you, consult an attorney first.

If you're 110% sure you want to leave you could approach your boss or Human Resources and ask for a severance package. If they were "considering" firing you, this might be a good out for them and they might readily agree. Beware: By accepting this you'll, most likely, have to sign away any future rights to sue them. Depending on the severance amount, severity of hating, and evidence you've amassed, it may or may not be worth it. Good news: In some states you can get a severance package and it won't affect your ability to collect unemployment.

Staying and suffering won't earn you a reward. No one's tombstone or obituary reads "died of a heart attack due to a female coworker constantly harassing her, but she is a real trooper for staying at the job and doing nothing". Staying there prolongs the situation. Leaving expresses the severity of the situation. It enables you to get out of the situation and move on with your life. Even if you do leave, don't expect the memories to go away overnight. Talking about it will help. Discuss it with your coworkers, other targets, family, and friends. It helps to know you're not alone.

Take some time out and grieve. Even if hating is no longer a factor there's nothing wrong with grieving. I spent six months trying to move up at the French pharmaceutical company I worked for. When I finally realized I'd have to leave and go elsewhere to get a job in Human Resources, I spent the whole weekend at home crying, but I came to terms with what I had to do and started applying to jobs outside my company. Grieve—you owe it to yourself.

Heaven

Heaven, age 34, took a summer job as a Human Resources clerk. The job was a six-month summer seasonal position at a beach town community with the possibility of becoming permanent. The person prior to her had become permanent after six months. Two years later that employee had been promoted, which was why the position was open.

On Heaven's first day she met the woman she was replacing, whom Heaven referred to as 'The Nervous Breakdown Lady'. The lady, who was in her fifties, wanted to do anything BUT train her. If Heaven had never worked in an office before she swore to me that she would have changed careers altogether. However, she had and she knew they weren't supposed to be run that way.

Heaven's office was unorganized and she soon found out there was a high turnover rate in her department. The nervous breakdown lady was more than happy to share that information with Heaven and the other new employees. She told Heaven that their boss was on medication and seeing a counselor. "She has a tendency to snap and bite peoples' heads off" were her exact words to Heaven. What annoyed Heaven most was how someone in the Human Resources department would say something so unprofessional, especially to new team members. Heaven instantly knew she had to watch out for this "friendly, oversharing coworker". But Heaven kept her mouth shut—a mistake?

What was more amazing was that the nervous breakdown lady couldn't even train Heaven, because she didn't even *know* her former position. How was Heaven supposed to learn it if the prior employee was incompetent and unknowledgeable? Heaven said, "Half the time it was like the blind leading the blind. She didn't know how to make photocopies, use the stamp machine, order office supplies, send a FedEx, or order business cards. I honestly didn't know what this woman had done over the past two years. I nicknamed her the nervous breakdown lady due to my boss. My second week there, when I asked my boss if my coworker would be available to train me, she told me that my coworker was having a nervous breakdown and would be going home. When I asked if she'd be returning, my boss said that she didn't know and that she didn't have enough time to train me."

Not only was the nervous breakdown lady incompetent at her former position, but she couldn't do her new one either. Thus, she manipulated people into doing her work by acting like she was their BFF, stabbed people in the back, constantly tried to get out of doing work, always talked about her personal life, and consistently needed to come into work late and leave early—and these were just *some* of her "redeeming qualities".

The nervous breakdown lady used her likeability factor to find unsuspecting people to do her bidding. She would flatter others in an effort to get them to do her work for her, thereby allowing her more time to socialize or not be present at her job due to something happening with one of her kids. She had their poor unsuspecting boss wrapped around her manicured little finger. As for the suspecting targets like Heaven, they were quickly disposed of.

The nervous breakdown lady was setting Heaven up to fail. She had a passive-aggressive, indirect, and dishonest style of dealing with Heaven. She "pretended" to be nice while sabotaging her. She smiled to Heaven's face — all the while assassinating Heaven's reputation to their boss. Did she realize Heaven was on to her? That I don't know, but I suspect if she did it was one motive for her to get rid of her as quickly as she could.

One day, the nervous breakdown lady suggested that their entire Human Resources office complain to their boss's boss. Heaven refused. She knew the problem lay more with the nervous breakdown lady, not their boss. In addition, she felt bad for their boss. Their boss was under a lot of stress from doing her own job and that of the nervous breakdown lady too. Did Heaven going against her wishes and not complaining about her boss infuriate the nervous breakdown lady more? Did she feel that Heaven was against her by not following her lead?

Soon, she noticed her boss had stopped making eye contact with her. The nervous breakdown lady would go into the boss' office and shut the door. Heaven had a feeling that sometimes it was about her. Heaven never had a performance issue, as she was overqualified for her position. She had a feeling that the nervous breakdown lady was filling her boss' head with lies about her.

At some point Heaven realized that she needed to start documenting what went on, so she did. She started writing notes in German and saving them on her work computer. She figured they'd be safe if they were in another language. Unfortunately, her dismissal was so rushed that she didn't have time to print anything out. Five months into her job, she received the standard "it's not working out". By then she was so disgusted with the place that she no longer cared. She didn't even think that her boss would believe her if she were to tell her what went on behind closed doors there.

*Note: This story is a perfect example of why you should keep your paper trail on your home computer and **not** on your work one.*

"Much as we wish that people would change, if they don't have a meaningful incentive or motive for working well with others, they won't."
- Julie Jansen,
"You Want Me to Work with Who?"

Whose Fault is it Anyway?

Whose fault is hating? Is it the fault of multiple entities? Your college, for not teaching you the workplace survival skills that you needed to stay employed? Your company, for not having rules or not investigating your accusations? Congress and the President, for not putting laws into place to protect you? Human Resources, for not being more involved? Don't forget your hater, because she's the one responsible for her own actions. Whose job is it to maintain a psychologically safe workplace and keep the workplace hate-free?

It sounds like we are talking about a bunch of kids in high school, doesn't it? Adults are responsible for their own behavior, yet it seems we need to place the responsibility onto another adult in the workplace to ensure that "hating" is stopped. If we don't, we will have a full scale hating epidemic. But is placing the responsibility on others to control their behavior working? Is this what we need to do? Or is there a better solution available? Whose fault is it, anyway?

Government

The United States Supreme Court has made it clear that Title VII is not intended to be a general civility code for the workplace. In her dissent, Ginsburg wrote, "The ball is once again in Congress' court to correct the error into which this court has fallen and to restore the robust protections against workplace harassment the Court weakens today." (Huppke, 2013, p. 4) The federal government regulates other types of workplace abuse, yet they've chosen to ignore hating. As of 2018, there is no federal or state law that addresses hating in the workplace. As the 7th Circuit Court once said, "Title VII protects against discrimination, not personal animosity or juvenile behavior."

Many industrialized countries consider hating the same as physical violence. As we know, verbal abuse can have longer lasting consequences than physical abuse. If other countries have implemented laws that deal with workplace hating, then why can't—and hasn't—the United States? Is it because lawmakers have never experienced hating or know anyone who has? Maybe it's because more lawmakers are male than female, thus less likely to encounter it. Or maybe it's because they think it could never happen to them. Or maybe they believe that it doesn't even exist. Maybe lawmakers feel that passing a law would encourage frivolous lawsuits.

"The United States is behind the curve in addressing workplace bullying, which has been studied for more than two decades in Europe. In many other industrialized countries, workplace bullying is considered a violation of a worker's inherent right to dignity and the source of potentially serious health and safety problems that could negatively impact the economy." (Barnes p. 48-9) In most other countries, it is considered the employers' responsibility to provide a workplace free from harassment and conducive to work. Many European countries such as Denmark, Finland, Belgium, Germany, the UK, France, the Netherlands, Norway, Serbia, Sweden, and several Canadian provinces have laws prohibiting this conduct in the workplace. Sweden was the first country to pass a workplace bullying law. Finland's Occupational Health and

Safety Acts covers physical and psychological violence, including threats of violence, harassment, and bullying. Norway's Working Environment Act states that efforts to combat bullying are to be part of the systematic health and safety program in the workplace. France's Labour Code imposes an obligation on employers to prevent psychological harassment. Australia introduced the anti-bullying jurisdiction of the Fair Work Commission on January 1, 2014, which lets a worker in Australia who reasonably believes she or he has been bullied at work apply to the Fair Work Commission and if it's determined that bullying has occurred, be entitled to a remedy. In the state of Victoria, Australia, workplace bullying is even considered a crime. The United States has done nothing but ignore this problem.

In the United States, workplace bullying has been found to be four times more prevalent than sexual harassment. Despite these findings, an employee can still be a target of bullying in the workplace in the United States and have no legal recourse as state and federal laws generally do not cover acts of hating. As of 2018, hating itself does not violate Title VII or any other anti-discrimination law. Currently, someone cannot sue for being hated on. However, they can sue if they are hated on because they are disabled, pregnant, or another reason that falls within a protected class. According to Roy Mauer of SHRM (Society for Human Resource Management), "Employees can sue companies for creating a 'hostile work environment', which can include bullying as harassment, but the harassment usually is tied to a protected category, such as race, sex, religion or national origin. Anti-bullying advocates are pushing legislation to protect workers who are not in a protected class. Other countries- England, Sweden, Australia- already have such laws."

Without a law, companies in the United States will continue to ignore, not confront, and not acknowledge this type of negative behavior that goes on in the workplace.

The company/owner

Maybe some owners don't care, because it's never happened to them. Take a restaurant I hostessed at. The owners had had it for over 35 years. Clearly, they were out of touch with reality and what it's like to work for other people and not own your own place. As owners, and knowing only that, they didn't understand the full extent of the damage that fellow female coworkers could do to each other.

Human Resources and senior leadership can put into place all the hating policies and procedures they want, but if they aren't enforced and the individual isn't held accountable then all the policies in the world won't help the target. Companies must set the expectation that there are rules that need to be followed and that hating won't be tolerated. Companies need hating policies in place that, depending on the severity of the incident, can lead to corrective action or termination.

Companies need to practice what they preach by engaging in appropriate workplace behaviors. If parents can't get their morals and principals right, how can their kids? Responsibility starts from the top and should filter down. If the owner is involved with the day-to-day operations of the company she/he must be fair. No favoritism allowed.

Companies need to provide the essential components such as fair pay, benefits, and legitimate policies. However, they are also responsible for equipping Human Resources with the tools and resources to help managers. Equipping managers, who work with the individuals each day, is essential. Without the support of the employer, it's difficult for Human Resources to manage hating situations.

Senior leadership

Setting the tone for a hate-free workplace should firstly stem from the leaders of the company. They are responsible for distributing key messages, modeling appropriate behaviors, and reinforcing policies that address hating. A positive, energetic, and supportive work environment starts at the top. They set the attitude about values and beliefs. They need to show support and commitment in keeping the workplace free from hating. Senior leadership plays a role in enforcing the culture and pushing away behaviors or acts that lead to hating.

Senior leadership needs to exhibit professionalism and ethics. A good leader doesn't take part in or tolerate hating. If senior leadership presents a solid message stating that hating isn't allowed, there's a good chance people will follow the leader. Leadership is a hat you never take off. Employees watch and mimic the behavior of senior leaders. If the message of what behaviors are appropriate aren't communicated, they will never be demonstrated by the employees.

Senior leaders need to create an open-door policy for hating. They need to be open to listening and encourage employees to approach them. Perhaps you have a better relationship with the Vice-President of your department than your direct manager or Human Resources Manager. If speaking to her/him about your hater makes you more comfortable and less hesitant to come forward, then it should be encouraged.

Company culture

Some corporate cultures not only accept women hating other women, but they also promote it. Is it a culture of mistrust? Fear? Are things not communicated? Is there a lack of team goals? Is bad behavior informally rewarded by the manager? By the company? Do managers engage in hating? If there's a lot of hating going on in your company, it's because your workplace has a culture that supports it. Companies encourage hating when they give excessive work, set unrealistic deadlines, perpetuate role confusion, are unorganized, set unattainable goals, or encourage competition among coworkers. Companies with tension, distrust, animosity, job stress, job insecurity, change, and fear can lead to hating. A culture with little clarity that leaves you constantly guessing promotes hating. When employees aren't clear about instruction they may be more apt to engage in hating, which ultimately impacts their work, the work environment, and professional relationships. Employees with clear instructions are less likely to engage in hating and more likely to enjoy their work. When things are stressful at work, people become aggressive.

The culture in the organization is set by key members within. It's their responsibility to be vigilant and address hating once it surfaces. They should solicit the help of Human Resources to put a plan in place that will deal with those that choose to engage in hating. It's important to send a message to employees that hating won't be tolerated. Employers must hold employees accountable for their actions towards other employees. This means that management must be ready to make the difficult decision when necessary and terminate the hater regardless of her position and tenure. It isn't enough to do a good job; employees must be team players. They must have their coworkers' backs and not be out to get them fired.

Human Resources and senior leadership need to create a culture that is trained to handle "issues" when they occur. A company is like a family. Not everyone is going to get along all of the time. When issues arise, they need to be dealt with—ignoring them isn't going to make them go away. Policy, law, or not—management needs to be proactive when they see signs of hating.

Company culture should be instilled in employees to show what is tolerated and what isn't. The best form or prevention is the establishment of a workplace culture and climate where anti-social and disruptive behaviors are not tolerated and result in serious consequences for perpetrators.

Your direct manager

Most people approach their manager first, for fear of "going over his head". Another reason, employees may be more apt to turn to their direct manager, whom they know better, for assistance is that some employees may "fear"

Human Resources. Perhaps they view Human Resources in a disciplinary light or they don't think their hating is detrimental enough to "bother" them. Going to your manager is a good place to start, because she/he might already have a handle on the current hating situation, or, if you're new to the company you may discover they understand the hater's troubles/history of hating. When an employee brings something to their manager, she/he is responsible and needs to intervene in the hating. If she/he isn't "competent" enough to do so then she/he needs to consult with her/his manager or involve Human Resources. Once someone comes forward, the incident must be resolved – and resolved quickly.

The work environment is set by whatever your manager allows to happen. The manager must take full control and own the department to ensure hating is stopped before consequences occur. Direct managers need to meet with their staff on a regular basis to reinforce the tone that hating won't be tolerated. The role of the manager is paramount in checking on the team's pulse on a day-to-day basis so that anything that can potentially lead to a future hating situation is nipped in the bud. Hating occurs because your direct manager chooses to look the other way and not get involved. When hating between coworkers starts, managers need to immediately address it. When hating is ignored by the supervisor it is reinforced. Remember the mean girl in elementary school that would tease you when there was a substitute? She's now your hater when your manager's back is turned.

When a manager loses focus, hating can take place. Managers are responsible for keeping employees focused and on task rather than engaging in hating. Managers play a central part in workplace relations by picking up on small issues that might escalate. Being on top of the hating and knowing the facts will help determine who is in trouble and who isn't. Managers need to keep tabs on the hating- they should consult with Human Resources, but they need to be able to manage their employees on their own too. The manager, with guidance from Human Resources, needs to accept responsibility for coaching the hater towards more constructive behavior.

Managers need to take responsibility in their work areas to make sure policies are followed. Human Resources may write the policies, perform the training, and set the tone in onboarding, but they may not be aware of issues unless management brings it to their attention. Human Resources, in most companies, is hidden away in their own wing. They aren't witnesses to the day-to-day interactions between employees. Direct managers are. Employees take direction and modify their behavior based upon the expectations and directions of their manager. When bad behavior is condoned or ignored by the manager, it is reinforced. Likewise, good behavior when reinforced and recognized by the supervisor, will increase.

Human Resources

Human Resources is typically viewed as the expert and therefore needs to lead in the effort to eliminate hating. Human Resources should, from time to time, meet with managers to make sure there are no concerns. Human Resources needs to take the initiative, along with managers, to make sure that everyone is on task, focused, and not engaging in hating.

Even the most effective managers can only do so much, as it impacts only their direct team. Human Resources' job is to transform the environment and culture of the company by having effective policies in place. Human Resources needs to be firm in disciplining hating and other types of behaviors that go against employees' well-being. Human Resources needs to enforce policies, ethics, and best business practices.

Human Resources is responsible for handling employee relations issues. They are there to deal with the drama so managers can deal with running the business and day-to-day operations. In a healthy company a competent Human Resources professional should be able to keep the lid on any hating and perhaps improve employee relations in the process. If the Human Resources representative isn't doing this it could be because she/he is unaware of the situation, the company won't back her/him up, senior leadership has told her/him to look the other way, or she/he is incompetent and not capable of doing her/his job.

Human Resources is the watchdog making sure that nothing comes back to hurt the company. That's what they are trained for. That being said, they can't rectify something they don't know about. Human Resources needs to be visible. Literally. I once had a manager who went on vacation for a week. She asked me to patrol her area twice a day to check for cellphone usage and to write up all offenders. Human Resources needs to get out and be seen.

Your hater

Your hater needs to take responsibility for her own actions. She needs to own the hating she brings to the workplace. Bottom line- each individual is responsible for their own behavior and needs to be held accountable. You don't have to like everyone you work with, but that doesn't mean you need to make their lives hell or get them fired.

We are adults not children and need to act accordingly. This is the workplace not an elementary school playground. Your hater should know that she can't act out and engage in hating in the workplace. WTH is she thinking anyway?

The females who befriend the hater and let her get away with it

When you're friends with a hater you become part of the problem. Even if you aren't actively engaged in hating, you are choosing not to be part of the solution via complicity and support of the hater's actions.

Why would you event want to be friends with a hater? WTH! Do you plan to look the other way or laugh when the hater engages in hating behavior? Even if you're not her target, do you really want to associate with this person? ENOUGH SAID.

Your college

Per my earlier chapter, you paid good money to go to college and learn your chosen profession. You may have even had internships. You would have thought that at some point along the way someone would have *mentioned* and *prepared* you for what the actual workplace would be like. But no one did. Shame on them.

Everyone

As responsible adults in the workplace, we should be able to expect that each person can monitor themselves. Unfortunately, we know that isn't true. Just as it takes a village to raise a child, it takes everyone in the workplace to keep the hating out. And by everyone I do mean everyone— managers, Human Resources, senior leadership, employees at all levels. In other words, the company as a whole. Everyone is responsible for establishing, modeling, and reinforcing a no hating culture. Employees should hold themselves accountable for practicing behaviors that contribute to a positive, hate-free environment.

We all have a part to play in shutting down hating, whether it's by coming forward and complaining when you're a target, whether it's intervening when one of your female coworkers' hates on another, writing to Congress to get laws passed, or by confronting the hater. Until more people step up and "get involved" and stop looking the other way, it won't end. It will continue on and on and on and…you get the picture. We need to step up when another female engages in hating; we need to set her straight and put her in her place. If we all took a proactive approach, the hater would lose her audience and be afraid of embarrassing herself, placing her own job in jeopardy, and being called on her hating behavior.

Everyone must play a role in minimizing tensions which create "workplace dramas". Just as we are responsible for our own actions, we are responsible for our own reactions. If you see hating, report it. Get involved. Don't walk away and "forget" about it. Employees are in a far better position than managers and HR to witness hating. Choose to be part of the solution- if you see hating, speak up and don't let her get away with it. You never know — it could be you next.

Corinne

I connected with Corinne on LinkedIn. Her hater, the senior most employee at her work, had been the person assigned to train her when she started her last job. Unfortunately, it appeared that she felt threatened by her. Her hater was extremely overweight, going through a nasty divorce, and on edge all the time. Corinne tried hard to get along with her even though their personalities were very different. Corinne considered herself upbeat. In addition, she was a newlywed and worked hard to stay slim. Whenever Corinne asked her to train her on tasks she needed to do, her hater would refuse to communicate with her. Often, she would outright ignore her. Corinne knew this woman was sabotaging her and setting her up to fail, not helping her.

How did Corinne handle the situation? She didn't. Corinne "assumed" it would fix itself. She ignored the situation and looked the other way. She figured it would pass. It didn't. Corinne was eventually terminated for not being able to do her new job. The job that she was never properly trained for. Afterwards she ran in to some of her former coworkers having lunch. They told her that her hater had done that to other people, but they had "handled" her. They told Corinne that she was too nice. Corinne confided to me, "I have to be who I am, and I'm not an evil tattle tale, or a jealous spirited person. I had no idea what to do or how to handle it, and I still don't know what I could have done differently."

Fannie

I connected with Fannie on LinkedIn. Fannie had lost her Dad a few years back. After she returned from bereavement she had a hard time coping. Her coworker, Krystale, told her that her supervisor had requested she take a few extra days off, because she was overwhelmed with grief. Fannie quickly left, in tears, but relieved. When she returned to work again she was written up and put on probation for not having her time off approved. Fannie's supervisor stated that she never approved the additional time away.

Fannie confronted Krystale. Krystale feigned innocence and claimed that she never told Fannie that their supervisor wanted her to take additional time. She said that perhaps Fannie was "confused" and should seek counseling. After Fannie confronted Krystale, things only got worse. Her supervisor started giving her odd looks. Fannie knew she was being talked about. Still overwrought with grief she went out on FMLA. She used that time to find a new job and never returned to her previous one.

"If it takes a village to raise a child, then most certainly it takes an organization working together to change the tide of toxicity."
- Marie-France Hirigoyen, "Stalking the Soul: Emotional Abuse and the Erosion of Identity"

Employer Accountability- the Solution?

While many companies do not condone hating, they ignore it when it happens. If your company won't look out for your best interests and stop the hating, then who will? Organizations are responsible not only for how they treat their employees, but also how their employees treat each other. You count on, as you should, your employer for doing what's morally right. What if you came to work and decided to only do "some" of your work from now on? Isn't that what employers are doing to targets of hating in a round-about way? They are saying, "Okay, we will give you a title and salary, but whatever else happens is up to you to fix."

Many talented females suffer due to not being able to deal with their female coworkers. Not everyone is able to manage how their female coworkers treat them. And why should they be able to? "The fact is that it was your employer who set the stage for the bully to operate as a loose cannon, failed to constrain him or her when told about it, and made you fend for yourself, isolated at work. The true culprit is the employer, and you never could have taken on that reform task alone." (Namie and Namie, 2009, p. XII).

Employees are entitled to expect that their coworkers will treat each other with a minimal level of common decency. They are entitled to expect that when that doesn't happen, their employer will intervene. They are entitled to expect that when they have a valid complaint, it will be investigated and the person at fault will be punished. Employees should NOT have to fear for their life, sanity, livelihood, physical health, or emotional well-being, because their company doesn't care and won't do anything to stop the hating. Companies need to be held accountable for what goes on during the course of the workday. Whether in the office or working from home on a Friday night, employers need to intervene. If they don't, then they need to be held accountable for not doing their part.

When hating is reported employers have four choices: Do nothing, punish the hater, fire the target, or promote/reward the hater. Unfortunately, most opt to do nothing. When companies don't put a stop to hating, they are condoning it. Companies might as well make a policy that states "hating is tolerated here". Companies who do nothing are just asking to be sued—so why not give them what they want? "Once a target complains to an employer that she is being abused, the employer has a legal obligation to act immediately to stop the abuse. Failure to act can expose the employee to significantly greater liability in a lawsuit." (Barnes p. 70-71). When companies let haters get away with things they are only putting themselves at risk. They are opening themselves up to lawsuits and a volatile work environment. It will come down to the company in the end. The company is at fault—not lawmakers. The target won't be suing them- she'll be suing the company. If you've complained and nothing has been done, then please stop reading this book and find yourself a good employment law attorney ASAP. I'm sorry, but your company deserves to be sued.

Even employers that do acknowledge there's a problem, tolerate it or just talk about it, neither of which *fixes* it. They don't want to deal with it and brush it under the rug. Some managers may even try minimizing your hater's behavior by offering up an excuse. Phrases like *she's just having a bad day* OR *she's going through something at home*, are ways management may justify *her* behavior and *their* inaction. Yes, they know it's going on, but they take the attitude, "It's your problem. Go figure it out." When I brought my situation to the attention of the President of the Board of Education, he acknowledged that, yes, new employees were hazed, but that they hadn't figured out how to handle it. "Doing nothing is not a neutral act when an individual explicitly asks for help. When nothing is done, the employer becomes the bully's accomplice, either deliberately or inadvertently, by allowing it to continue unabated." (Namie and Namie, 2009, p. 11). Management needs to understand that ignoring hating doesn't make it go away. In fact, quite the opposite occurs — it usually escalates.

Common reasons companies and management ignore hating:

- Males in management see hating as something females do and chalk it off as "women will be women". They have the "let them fight it out" mentality.
- They are in denial that hating occurs, because they don't believe that an employee would deliberately set out to destroy another team member.
- They don't care.
- They can't comprehend it, because it's never happened to them.
- They don't understand how bad it is.
- They don't know what to do.
- They feel it's a waste of their time to get involved and don't want to be bothered with it.

- They feel that their employees are adults and should be able to resolve their differences without involving management.
- They feel that they don't have the money or manpower to devote to hating. "The idea that companies do not have the time or financial wherewithal to deal with problems among female coworkers is shamefully shortsighted. In downplaying or dismissing such problems, they are losing employee time and energy that should be extended to the job itself. And they are losing employees." (Mooney, 2006, p. 224).
- They see it as a normal and acceptable way to behave.
- They think that by ignoring the problem someone will quit.
- They think that the target asked for it.
- They think/hope it will fix itself.

Do companies not understand that when someone complains and they rectify the hating situation, that there's less of a chance they will get sued? Do they not understand that by doing nothing it opens them up to a lawsuit? Do they not understand that doing something could decrease employee turnover and increase employee morale? Do they not understand that a happy employee is a loyal employee? Do companies not understand that hating causes them to lose some of their best workers? Do they not understand the cost in terms of retention, training, and recruitment? Did they eat stupid for breakfast or are they just in plain denial? Companies shouldn't allow this type of behavior, yet they do.

By not having a hating policy in place, companies give the impression that they don't want to solve the problem. Schools have anti-bullying policies for students, so why shouldn't the workplace? Why don't they make and enforce policies that protect their employees? Do most companies care so little about their employees' welfare at work? Do most business owners not have a conscience? Or are the people at the top too far removed from what's going on in their own company? Shouldn't companies seek to avoid possible lawsuits and understand they encourage them by not having policies against hating? If I owned a company, it would bother me immensely if employees were forced to quit due to hating by their coworkers. Wouldn't you feel the same?

I don't understand why employers allow hating in the workplace. Create and enforce policies—it's not rocket science. You can't stop people from talking and doing what they really want to do. However, if there are consequences and people are held accountable for their behavior, it might help deter them.

Potential consequences for employers

Hating can turn a positive working environment into a climate of fear and distrust. It can turn coworker against coworker. Good employees leave, the employer's reputation becomes tarnished, and they are unable to recruit talented workers.

When a female hates on another female she is putting her own interests ahead of the company's. This behavior shouldn't be tolerated, yet it's become accepted and the norm. Companies seem to FORGET THAT ALL THIS

NEGATIVE BEHAVIOR AFFECTS PRODUCTIVITY, EMPLOYEE MORALE, AND TURNOVER. According to the Workplace Bullying Institute, "37% of workers have been bullied. Yet many employers ignore the problem, which hits the bottom line in turnover, healthcare, and productivity, costs, the institute says." How can this type of environment be comfortable to work in, much less conducive to getting work done? Less work gets done when targets are worried about their job. It's hard to be productive when you're constantly looking over your shoulder. Why do companies NOT realize this?

How much money does the United States spend a year due to hating? While I have no exact number, according to author Patricia Barnes, "It's in the billions" — money spent on unemployment, welfare, disability, and other social programs. Don't forget the banks that lose money when hating targets can't pay their mortgage, car loan, and credit cards.

Employers need to realize that hating has immense costs, both financially and emotionally, on both the target and the workplace. It doesn't make good business sense for companies to look the other way and allow hating. It doesn't make good business sense for companies not to have policies against hating. It doesn't make good business sense for haters to remain part of the team. It doesn't make good business sense to fire the target in an attempt to get rid of the problem.

Potential consequences for employers:
- Increased absenteeism.
- Employee complaints.
- Tension.

- Low/decrease in employee morale.
- Money lost from work not being done: Over-time, temp help.
- Emotional toll it takes on target and those who witness it.
- Investigation that costs time and manpower.
- Third party harassment lawsuits.
- Increased costs in recruiting.
- Learning curve for new employees.
- Increase in breaks.
- Loss of profit.
- Bad publicity and harm to the company's reputation.
- Needless turnover- "A 2007 study for the Level Playing Field Institute of San Francisco, CA, a non-profit group that promotes fairness in the American workplace, estimates that more than two million professionals and managers in the United States are pushed out of their jobs each year by cumulative small comments, whispered jokes, not-so-funny emails, etc. The Institute estimates the cost of this needless turnover at $64 billion a year." (Barnes p. 98).
- Decrease in productivity. "The Workplace Bullying Institute estimates that turnover and lost productivity due to aggressive behaviors in the workplace could cost a single Fortune 500 company as much as $24 million a year- plus $1.4 million in litigation and settlement costs." (Barnes p 98).
- Cost of consultants.
- Legal fees.
- Settlement costs.

- Cost of unemployment insurance claims.
- Cost of workers' comp claims.
- Cost of disability claims.
- Increase in health insurance premiums.
- Increase in premiums for short-term disability, long-term disability, and employee assistant programs.
- Transfer requests.
- Loss of skill and experience when the target leaves due to hating.

Companies *should* realize that anti-hating laws would be beneficial to them. It would decrease lawsuits. This would save companies' money and time. It would increase productivity. There is a strong correlation between individual well-being and business results. Negative remarks and comments aren't constructive to the business environment. Whether it results in making mistakes or working less effectively, you can expect your work to suffer as it becomes secondary to the impacts of hating. Laws would allow employees to be less worried about their hater and more worried about the work on their desk, not to mention less turnover. A lot of time and energy goes into hiring and training someone new. For example: Once I knew Sayreville was terminating me I had three and a half months left to work. I had approximately 17 sick days and you can bet I used every one of them. Sayreville, at the time, paid $90 a day to substitute teachers. You do the math. Turnover is not cheap. Roughly estimated it is about 30-50% of the salary of the person you are replacing. Whether it's taking time to conduct interviews or paying employees overtime to pick up the slack, turnover is costly. While I left Sayreville without a settlement, it cost time and money to replace me. My replacement left. It cost time and money to replace my replacement. Then the following teacher also left, so more time and money was put into my former position. Such a waste of time and money; money that could have been used for textbooks or activities that could have increased enrollment in French.

The solution

During the recession I worked at two diners. They were as different as night and day. The second diner was run well. There was always at least one manager on. Employees were closely monitored. There was even an employee manual with rules, expectations, and consequences. Employees who acted out were spoken to or fired. This helped to maintain an orderly establishment that was harassment-free. If a small business with NO HUMAN RESOURCES department can do it, then a big company with several hundred people in their Human Resources department has no excuse.

Companies need to have a protocol to handle hating. They need to have strategies and plans to deal with it. They need to educate themselves that, yes, it exists, and they need to position themselves to intervene when it occurs. They need to establish rules, put them in writing, and live by them. The latter being the most important. There's no point in having rules if they aren't enforced. Management needs to hold the hater accountable for her behavior. If all else fails THEN THIS PERSON NEEDS TO BE FIRED! Do not pass GO, do not collect $200. This will show other haters that this type of behavior isn't accepted at this company. Companies need to have a zero-tolerance policy.

Having policies and enforcing them can help companies be successful, productive, and profitable. There needs to be a clearly written policy that prohibits hating, bullying, employee abuse, and a hostile work environment. Develop a staff code of conduct that defines acceptable and unacceptable behaviors. Include a NO HATING HERE CLAUSE in the employee handbook. SHRM recommends the following language: (Company Name) defines bullying as repeated inappropriate behavior, either direct or indirect, whether verbal, physical, or otherwise, conducted by one or more persons against another or others, at the place of work and/or in the course of employment. Such behavior violates (Company Name) Code of Ethics which clearly states that all employees will be treated with dignity and respect. By having policies against hating, companies let employees know that hating isn't acceptable in the workplace. If companies refuse to tolerate hating, it will stop. Include a policy that any employee terminated for hating (with cause) will have their unemployment denied. Why not? Companies can have any policies they want as long as they are legal, do not discriminate, and are business related.

Companies are not only responsible for having anti-hating policies and investigating hating accusations, but also for who they hire (the hater). Companies need to spend time and money finding the right candidate. They need to make hiring the right candidate, aka not a hater, a priority. The company owes it to all employees to hire non-haters. The recruitment process needs to take into account the dynamics of group personalities and future interactions. It's important to hire someone who's a good fit for the company. It needs to be as much about hiring non-haters as it is about hiring competent and skilled professionals. Human Resources should have the basic knowledge of reading people and their personalities, so they can hire the right people to help minimize conflict. Obviously, no hater is going to disclose her hating past during the interview process. She won't be wearing a sign on her shirt- but yet Human Resources hired her. Perhaps a better screening process? A more extensive background check? Was she an employee referral? Perhaps a change in advertising boards is needed if your company seems to only attract haters.

Companies need to have training in place. You can hire the most knowledgeable and well-educated people, but if you don't train them, what good will they be? Provide new hires with a thorough overview of the company's rules, expectations, policies, procedures, and ethics. Ensure that employees receive proper training on how to behave and communicate in the workplace through regular orientation and re-orientation processes. Develop (better) training and programs on hating. Companies need to communicate expectations from orientation all the way through day-to-day chats, demonstrating appropriate behavior at ALL LEVELS, and recognize those who do engage in responsible, mature workplace behavior.

Managers need to be better prepared to handle hating situations. Managing employees is no easy feat and it can be one of the most challenging functions any manager can face. Companies need to train managers on handling hating incidents and how to respond to complaints. As most managers are more skilled in their subject than dealing with people, they may need additional training or be prepared to refer them to someone in Human Resources to handle it.

Managers need to understand their role in preventing and addressing hating. Managers that look the other way and do nothing need to be held accountable for their actions. Yes, this includes termination.

Companies need to involve Human Resources—that's why they're there. Human Resource managers are trained to investigate, interview, and respond to incidents, so why not let them do their job? Hating needs to be documented, especially when the target falls within a protected class. HR can recommend termination, discipline, or coaching. If Human Resources can't handle it, then they need to bring in an outside consultant, coach, or call an employment lawyer. In most companies, HR is also responsible for exit interviews. They're a great tool to see what's really going on in a specific department. At that point—the employee has little to nothing to lose in coming forward and outing her hater or someone else's.

Employers need to stop hating when it's reported. They need to be proactive by stepping in and intervening in an EFFECTIVE manner. When Human Resources or managers receive information that hating is occurring, they need to investigate and determine what's really going on. The person at fault needs to be punished. When employers do nothing, they need to be held accountable for their failure to remedy the situation. Companies are responsible for what happens over the course of the workday and companies who ignore hating should be fined and penalized.

No sane person would want to work at a company where hating occurs and is accepted. Even if you're not the target, it's a toxic environment. All employees have the right to work in a positive work environment, free from hating. If this is not the case, it is the employer's responsibility TO DO SOMETHING ABOUT IT. If the United States isn't going to step up and pass a law, then companies need to come up with a protocol for handling it. If they don't, it serves them right when they get sued.

Savannah

Savannah started a new job at a large well-known coffee chain. One of her female coworkers, Jane, took an instant dislike to her. Savannah could not understand why, but assumed this woman was taking her anger out on her. Jane's husband had recently left her for a younger woman and as a result Jane had lost her house, and was forced to drop out of college and go back to work. She started by bad mouthing Savannah and spreading rumors about her. She would blame Savannah for various problems that had nothing to do with her — everything from the copy machine breaking to the Fedex man arriving late. She'd undermine her to get her in trouble. She would yell and talk down to Savannah. Because Jane was mean and treated lots of people poorly, Savannah didn't take it personally. Savannah was young and told me she didn't know any better, so she overlooked it in the beginning.

However, it persisted and worsened. Savannah became stressed and started losing weight. She never knew what she would be walking into the next day and started dreading going to work. One day she woke up and couldn't breathe. She went to the doctor, who examined her and told her that she was having a panic attack. He sent her to a psychologist who explained to her that she was being targeted and advised her to quit her job. Thankfully a better opportunity came up and she was able to do so.

Jen

Jen, 35, took a hostess job at a small well-known local diner. Kelsey, a waitress, told Jen after a few days that Jen was doing an excellent job and that she had reported exactly that to management. To the average inexperienced worker, that may have sounded like a compliment—how thoughtful of Kelsey. She didn't have to go out of her way to tell management that Jen was doing a good job. Jen, however had plenty of work experience and knew how to interpret it—"Basically, she was telling me that she had influence and just as easily as she told them that I was doing a good job-she could tell them that I was doing a bad job."

After several weeks Jen and Kelsey had a run-in, which resulted in Kelsey going to management. Kelsey claimed that Jen wasn't seating her properly and she was losing money when Jen hostessed. On paper, Jen had done everything correctly. Perhaps Kelsey was having a bad day? Perhaps Kelsey had had some bad tippers and wanted to blame her lack of money on Jen? Perhaps Jen really did make mistakes regarding seating? All Jen knew was that her blood pressure was up and her stress level was raised, thanks to Kelsey. Management started to look at Jen and doubt her capability. It seemed to Jen that Kelsey was out to sabotage her. She didn't understand why. She didn't want Kelsey's job. Why would Kelsey want to get rid of her, if that's what she wanted?

Jen learned a few things. It seemed like Kelsey was threatened by her. As the youngest waitress, she got lots of attention and didn't like it that Jen was younger. Jen had more going for her and was more educated. Kelsey had six kids, was struggling financially, and probably had little control in her own life. In addition, her fourteen year old daughter, who also hostessed there, had lost some of her hours when Jen started. Perhaps, Kelsey was prejudiced against Jen from the start. It seemed like Kelsey thought that she was in charge and could heavily influence management. It seemed like she even wanted, at one point, to have Jen fired so she could show everyone the control she had at the restaurant. Whatever the excuse, Kelsey's behavior caused Jen unneeded stress.

The first time Kelsey confronted Jen, she was surprised by Kelsey's loud, rude, and aggressive behavior. She wrote if off as a misunderstanding and thought that maybe Kelsey was having a bad day (again). One day, Kelsey pushed the clipboard Jen was holding in an aggressive manner, which inadvertently pushed her. (Can we say hostile workplace, lawsuit waiting to happen?) Jen was in shock after she did this and yelled at her for seating her table. (Honestly, isn't the whole point of waitressing to get tables sat to make money?) Shocked, she went back to her hostess stand. Again, she could feel her blood pressure rising.

She mulled over her non-action and regretted not confronting her. She was angry that this waitress thought she could run the restaurant and control who worked there. The waitresses thought they owned and ran the restaurant, even though much of this was the owners' fault as they let them get away with it. The waitresses thought they could do whatever they wanted and get away with it, because they had in the past.

The third time Kelsey confronted Jen, in a roomful of customers, Jen was ready for her. This time when she was pushed, she was ready for her attacker and verbally assaulted her back. Jen knew she would never be able to please this individual. She was never happy. Either she wasn't getting enough tables, had too many tables, there weren't enough people at the table, or it was too close to leaving time and she didn't want a big table... The list went on. She was always in the right—at least in her mind.

After Kelsey stood up to her she never pushed her clipboard again. However, Kelsey opted to leave anyway. She didn't need the stress in her life.

"Guys have a fight. There's a punch. It's over. Girls don't fight fair. They gang up. They keep secrets. Plot. They cut you down with a look."
-Noel Kahn,
Pretty Little Liars

Top 25 Things College Should Teach You to Help You Stay Employed

I was originally aiming for the top "10" things, but when I started to write this chapter I realized how important it was and ended up with 25. When I polled this question on Facebook the majority of my friends were confused. One responded, "Subject matter". Another, "Weathering economic downturns, being adaptive to changes in the job market, small business basics." Another, "I don't think it's a college's job to teach somebody how to keep a job." In an ideal world, sure. And maybe this all holds true for men, but if you've gotten this far in this book you know it's not true for women. With that in mind, here are the top 25 things college *should* teach you to help you stay employed:

1. **A positive working relationship with your fellow female coworkers is just as, if not more, important than the rapport you have with your boss.** Being happy, stress free, and not hated on by your fellow female coworkers' correlates to higher job satisfaction, productivity, and retention.

2. **Intuition. Get it? Got it? Good.** Listen to your feelings and intuition about what is happening to you and around you. A woman's intuition is her best friend. Do not dismiss a sixth sense that something is amiss. Gestures, tones, facial expressions, nonverbal clues, and the cease of chatter when you approach can be more truthful than words and can clue us in. For example: "Jane, were you just talking about me?" "Um…no you must have misunderstood…" stuttered while she looks down, looks guilty, doesn't make eye

contact, and searches for words. I once had a BFF who would look down and laugh each time she told a lie. Often when a lie fails, it's because a nonverbal sign of emotion was expressed. The bigger the lie, the harder it is to stifle the emotions associated with it. There's a reason "Laura" has a guilty look when she sees you. There's a reason "Christie" no longer eats lunch with you. There's a reason why the head of Human Resources has stopped saying hello to you. Your instinct will never steer you wrong. If it doesn't feel right, then it probably isn't. If you think that your female coworker is out to get you, then she probably is. If you feel like you're being hated on, then you probably are. Most people are taught to rely on facts and not to trust their gut instinct. Don't doubt yourself. You're your own best defense and greatest ally. Aim to be objective, but don't doubt yourself. You want to eat, sleep, and drink paranoia, forget everything negative you've ever heard about the word — it's your new BFF (next to yourself, of course!) Everyone is out to get you. Proceed with caution. Watch your back. Don't ever hesitate in questioning your female coworkers' intentions. There's nothing wrong in being overly cautious. Your intuition is a result of all the experiences, both good and bad, that you've had. It will guide you when something isn't right. Don't worry about appearing paranoid. If it seems like other women are preventing you from achieving your goals, trust me, they probably are. *Always trust your gut — it knows what your head hasn't figured out yet.*

3. **Beware of phony coworkers.** When starting a new job, be wary of the nice, wonderful coworker who befriended you on the first day. She was great—she showed you around, introduced you to everyone, and even took you out to lunch. She has nothing to gain by stabbing you in the back—or does she? If you think your female coworker is too good to be true, then she probably IS. Just because she may be smiling doesn't mean she doesn't have a hidden agenda. Ask yourself: What's in it for her?

4. **Expect the unexpected and be ready to roll with it.** Just like life doesn't always go as planned, your career won't either. Deal with it.

5. **Holding your own.** Knowing what to say, when to say it, how to say it, and whom to say it to becomes a crucial part of staying employed. Refusing to play the games that women in the workforce play will only result in you losing. You might as well just watch your career go up in flames. Hell, you might as well light the match yourself.

6. **Even though hard work, diligence, perseverance, intelligence, and a good education can all contribute to career success, it can all be railroaded by just one bitch.**

7. **Steer clear of toxic coworkers.** If you've seen a fellow female coworker stab another coworker in the back, keep in mind that you could be next. Leopards don't lose their spots. This person is definitely someone you want to avoid or you might find you're the next person taking the knife out of their back.

8. **Saying too much.** I **cannot** stress this point enough. Be careful what personal information you share with your coworkers. The coworker who is your friend today might not necessarily be your friend tomorrow. Revealing personal information on the job makes you vulnerable. As a rule of thumb never provide anyone information that can damage you. People will flatter you with attention and even buy you gifts to encourage you to open up and reveal information about yourself. They will wine and dine you with the hope that you may become quite loquacious after a few drinks. They may even pretend to be your friend or take an interest in your life, because their ulterior motive is to get personal information from you that they can use for their own benefit. Sad, but true. The "friendly" coworker at your new job might be upset that you got the position she applied for and she'll say anything to dig into your past and drag some skeletons out from you. Remember the book, *The Rules*? Pretend you're on a date with each coworker you meet. Guard your information with your life. Be mysterious and don't reveal too much about yourself. People love to talk about themselves—I know I do! Ask them questions to get them talking about themselves and get the focus off of you. **Just remember anything you say can and will be used against you at a later date.** When you share personal information at work you might as well be giving your coworkers a shovel to start digging your grave. It's the best way to sabotage yourself. You want to lose a job? Go in and tell your coworkers your life story—

they'll thank you by using it against you. You may not be able to control your coworker, but you can control what comes out of your mouth.

9. **One word, but I'm going to write it three times, because I can't stress it enough: Network. Network. Network.** If you aren't networking, then don't bother going to work. You never know who you'll meet and who they'll know or what they'll know. It's too late to network when you're getting escorted out the door by security. Don't wait until it's too late to form them. Start networking the day you start your new job. Build and maintain relationships. Take every opportunity to interact with others. Let your coworkers know the real you. Let them see you for the competent, professional, talented, personable, and friendly person that you are. Look for opportunities to work and interact with upper management. Mingle with them and other employees. When I was the receptionist of a large pharmaceutical company I spent a great deal of my day, every day, networking with the hundreds of employees and visitors that came through our doors daily. Network in the cafeteria at lunchtime. Network at company functions. Network in the bathroom. Say hello. Shake people's hands. Compliment them. Engage them in small talk. Social networking websites make this all 100x easier today than what it was 10 years ago. LinkedIn is your new BFF. If you don't have an account stop reading right now, create an account, then resume reading. LinkedIn is one of the best professional networking sites. You can use it to meet

other people in your company or connect with those you have already met. Get involved. My pharmaceutical company had a women's networking group, WISE (Women Inspiring Sanofi Employees). Not only did I join and go to events, I got involved by volunteering. At meetings, I would be a greeter and pass things out. Also any hobby you have is a good way to get involved and connect. At my pharmaceutical company we had an unofficial knitting club. Every other Thursday we'd sit in the cafeteria together and work on our projects. I only knew one person my first time, but over the months I got to know the whole group.

10. **Befriend the janitor, maintenance, receptionist, cleaning staff, and all the people at the "bottom" that the majority of folks can't be bothered with.** When I was an undergrad at Rider one of my education teachers, **Dr. Curran,** touched on this. So true. These people are important! They are privy to information that the majority of employees aren't. You need them as allies. Believe me, as most are ignored, they will be pleased with your genuine kindness and friendliness. When you need to know something, they'll be more likely to help a "friend" than someone high up on the rung. When I was a receptionist I was privy to information that people higher up weren't. I knew who was coming in late and leaving early, which married people were having affairs with each other, who was pretending to no longer be a smoker, and lots of other juicy details that the average employee didn't know. Trust me, these

people are some of the greatest allies you'll ever make.

11. **Be wary of sharing your new ideas with coworkers until you get to know them, trust them, and develop a working relationship with them.** There's nothing worse than a vicious backstabbing coworker who steals your ideas and assumes credit for them.

12. **Go out of your way to do your coworkers favors.** Whether it's asking if they need anything from the supply closet or giving up your parking spot for someone who sprained their ankle, GIVE. Do things to help someone. You never know when you'll need the favor returned.

13. **Smile**- even if you don't mean it. Smile when you greet each person. Smile when they greet you. Smile at the beginning of every conversation. It will be harder for someone to hate on you and fire you if you're always smiling.

14. **Make sure the people at the top know your name and who you are.** I wanted to eventually transition from my receptionist position to one in Human Resources. When Christmas came I made my famous Rice Krispie peanut butter balls. I dropped off a batch with the executive assistant of the Vice-President of Human Resources (Note: Dropping off food for him didn't get me a face-to-face with this busy man). To my surprise and pleasure, the following week he went out of his way to walk over to my receptionist desk to tell me how much **both he and his wife** enjoyed them. Of course, I did mention that I wanted to get into Human Resources (sure, why not?)

15. **Advance planning: Identify your opponents.** It's never too soon to plan. Unless you know you're going to be working in an all-male environment, it's something that will come up. If you work with a coworker who has a habit of making snide remarks to her coworkers, why not have a comment ready to go? **Be proactive.** Being prepared for your female coworkers is half the battle. Be proactive in looking out for people and situations that can harm you. Not everyone can think on the spot and have a ready answer. If you suspect a hater has chosen you as her next target it's time to act and act quickly. Usually, there's little you can do to stop the process once it's already under way. It's important to think before you act and know your options.

16. **Don't gossip.** We've all been talked about and gossiped about at some point in our life. If your coworkers don't hesitate in spreading gossip about others, beware: You could be next. However, this doesn't mean you shouldn't listen to gossip. For instance, if you walk into the bathroom and overhear an employee being trashed, you may secretly agree with the comments and assessments, but you can never let on.

17. **Be open minded to what your female coworkers have to say.** You may not always agree. Hell, you many never agree. But you need to be open-minded or at least present yourself as such. No one knows everything. Be open to learning.

18. **Hazing can and does take place in the workplace.** "Such harassment within groups of women can

transcend gentle prodding to become a powerful and threatening way of putting a newcomer in her place. This can prove especially true in situations in which women have few growth opportunities and little formal control, such jobs as sales clerks, secretaries, and certain low-level factory workers, jobs that are frequently female dominated." (Mooney, 2005, p. 195). Jobs today can make you feel like you're trying to pledge a sorority. Only this time with a twist of hating added to it.

19. **Be careful who you trust.** Especially if you're a woman trusting another woman. Generally, I don't trust people. If I want to tell a secret to someone that I really want to stay a secret, I tell my cat. Really. I know that trust is a touchy subject for lots of people. For me, trust is something that needs to be earned. I can't just meet someone and automatically trust them, just because they've never given me a reason not to. On the contrary, what have they ever done for me to trust them? I believe most people don't have my opinion and are less cautious, however just because she's your coworker, doesn't mean you should trust her. Doing so may come back to haunt you.

20. **You're not at work to make friends.** If it happens, great. But don't expect it or go looking for it. It's best to not mix your personal and your professional life. In fact, "making friends" can be one of the worst things you can do at a job. Maybe it's best to do what men do—approach each relationship at work with friendliness, but not with the intent to start a friendship. If a friendship forms over time, great. But

we're at work to work—not to cultivate our social circle. Your coworkers aren't your friends—they are your coworkers. If they were your friends they'd be called your friends and not your coworkers. Remember, it's your job that brought you together and your colleagues can easily take that away from you.

21. **Join a professional organization OUTSIDE of your company.** You'll be able to network there, get professional advice, hear others' stories, and be seen. This can help in the future when looking for a job.

22. **Be aware of workplace politics as they can determine career success.** Learn them. Memorize them. Respect them. Know the key players. Stay in touch with what is going on around you. Know whose alliance is to whom. You don't want to find out the person you use as your sounding board is your hater's workplace BFF.

23. **Life isn't fair.** The workplace isn't fair either. Don't expect to receive praise for hard work, get a promotion when you deserve one, or your female coworkers to play fair. The professionalism you'd think would exist in the workplace doesn't. The courtesy that others should extend to you won't be. Women can be vicious and the workplace is no exception.

24. **Don't let your female coworkers know your weaknesses.** Showing where you are vulnerable is as good as wearing a "Fire Me" shirt.

25. **Know when to cut your losses and move on.** Take everything with a grain of salt and decide that it

might just be your time to leave with your dignity intact. If your company doesn't appreciate you, then it's not the place for you. As my best friend, Allen Kalik, used to quote to me from the Kenny Rogers' song *The Gambler*, "You got to know when to hold, know when to fold up, know when to walk away, know when to run". What exactly does this mean? To stay employed you need to know when to start looking for a new job, when to save face by leaving on your terms, and how to work on getting a great recommendation.

Theresa

I connected with Theresa on LinkedIn. Like myself, she was also in the Human Resources field. In addition, she also had a MBA. Theresa believed her hater was threatened by her. Her hater refused to meet with her or include her in opportunities to help their department. Theresa felt completely compartmentalized. When she confided a weakness to her hater, she saw that as an opportunity to sabotage Theresa's career. She labeled Theresa as the problem and went on a campaign stating that Theresa was incompetent and unqualified to do her job. Theresa reported this to upper management, but received no support.

As management didn't intervene, her hater continued her campaign against Theresa. She was quick to point out a mistake Theresa made, even if someone else had made the same error. She spent her day monitoring Theresa, whether it was walking past her desk or asking coworkers' what Theresa was working on. Theresa felt like she always had an eye on her. This, of course, only caused Theresa to make more mistakes. She felt uneasy, had a nervous stomach, and felt anxious. This, in turn, made her start calling out sick — none of which helped her situation. Eventually she was terminated at the ninety-day mark as "not a good fit...not working out..." She had only her wonderful former coworker to thank for making her stand out and management for not caring.

Haleigh

I connected with Haleigh on LinkedIn. She worked in a medical practice, where the majority of her female coworkers were jealous of her due to her managerial position. Friendly with her at first, they used the "good working relationship" they had with her to their advantage. They'd ask her questions about what she was working on, meetings she had attended, and personal information about patients. As her work was confidential, she'd give vague answers, which never satisfied them. She caught a few of her female coworkers going through things in her office and viewing privileged information they shouldn't have been. Her female coworkers didn't hesitate in sharing what they found with others. After all, they wanted her to look bad so they could get rid of her. This caused her to be viewed in a different light by doctors and upper management. Not only did she see a difference in how management was treating her, but her coworkers would become silent when she would walk in the room. She became sullen and depressed. She ultimately left the position that she felt she had fought so hard to achieve.

Tina

I connected with Tina on Facebook. She'd been in therapy for three years and was in tears when she told me her story. Tina was the HR representative for a well-known retail chain. She had a female coworker, who for whatever reason had never liked her. Fortunately, Tina was friends with the store manager, who always kept her hater in check. One day the store manager was transferred. When this occurred, Tina was on FMLA leave, because her Dad was dying. She returned to work to find a new woman as store manager. Unfortunately, her hater had used Tina's leave as time to win over the new store manager and turn her against Tina. Tina returned, only to be attacked her first day back. Not only did her new store manager not intervene, but she joined in the hating. Her coworker accused her of not knowing her job. They wouldn't allow her to leave the office until she admitted she couldn't do her job properly. She insisted she could do her job and they kept arguing with her that she couldn't. She finally told them to send her to another store to get better training if they weren't happy. They did, but then they retaliated when she came back. Her hater would sit in the store manager's outer office to guard the door to prevent Tina from speaking with her. They would withhold information regarding store changes and anything else that she needed to do her job. They would page her to the store manager's office and time how long it took her to get there. Whenever she requested a day off, they would always give her a different day off. She was accused of changing people's time off from sick to temporary leave of absence, which is how it was supposed to be coded, to avoid firing people from using their sick time. They would go into the computer and change it back to sick. Once, they made her paint a room as punishment. When she'd do the new employee orientation, they would come in and interrupt her. She asked them repeatedly to stop, but this only increased their interruptions. One time they interrupted her 15 times in one day.

Tina contacted the corporate office, but they were of no help. They came out and interviewed her, but concluded they would do nothing as no wrong doing had occurred. Another employee, who witnessed some of this, called the 800 number and reported what she saw. Unfortunately, it was never investigated, because she did it anonymously. Tina never received a negative evaluation, until the very end when she was written up for poor job performance.

It impacted every area of her life. She contemplated suicide. She finally realized she just couldn't do it anymore when her store manager repeatedly had her move the bulletin board from one location and then back to its prior location. She quit without giving two weeks' notice. She handed them her resignation letter and badge and walked out, free at last. Unfortunately, she didn't have another job lined up, but she put in an unemployment claim (re: harassment) and they didn't fight it. She now suffers from Rheumatoid Arthritis and has PTSD from her hating experience.

"I am alarmed by the violence that other women do to each other: professional violence, competitive violence, emotional violence...I am alarmed by a growing absence of decency on the killing floor of professional women's worlds."

-Toni Morrison, Commencement Address Bernard College

The Future of Women in the Workplace

Imagine how great your job would be if you could get rid of the haters. Is it crazy to dream of a workplace environment free of women who take great pride in messing with other women's lives? To even become obsessed with this issue? Is a 100% hate-free workplace asking for too much? Are we wasting our time even thinking about how to end hating? Did I waste my time writing this book?

I do want to take the time to acknowledge that there are "some" good women out there; women who aren't out to get you fired or force you to quit. Women who don't care if you're doing well at work. Women who don't care if you get ahead. Women who don't care if you're well-liked, admired, or ambitious. Women who are team players and supportive of other women. Women who have no desire to try to hold someone back and keep them down. Women who know that by you getting ahead it could someday help them too. Unfortunately, these women are few and far between.

We work with women who focus on who has the better position, who is doing a better job, who dresses better — just to name a few. We work with women who do not address things up front and then let it go and move on. We work with women who worry way too much about what everyone else is doing. We work with women who constantly try to show off and prove who is better. We work with women who focus on sabotaging the careers of other women. We work with women who find and focus on the flaws in everything we do. We work with women who nip at the heels of other females, waiting for them to slip up, so they can profess their expertise. Who responds well to this type of behavior, may I ask? Shouldn't we all try to help each other? Why can't we all just get along?

Women *should* be looking out for other women...

but yet they aren't. We should be trying to help each other out. After all, it's taken decades to get us to where we are. Despite all the advances in women's rights, women still remain far behind men in the business world, both in regards to advancement and positions of importance and salary. For every $100 a male earns, a female earns $28 less. For every nine **male** vice-presidents in a company, there's only *one* **female** vice-president. Women still need better paying jobs, more opportunities for advancement, more workplace flexibility, and improved childcare options- to name a few. Although we've come a long way since the women's movement in the 1970s, true equality in the business world between men and women hasn't yet been attained.

It would be nice to work in an environment where your female coworkers are ethical, loyal, helpful, team players, committed, and out for the good of the company. In an ideal world an ideal workplace would exist. The work environment would be one of sympathy, trust, caring, empathy, communication, productivity, and teamwork. It would be an environment where people are not afraid of making mistakes for fear of being talked about and laughed at. Women would have each other's backs. We would be committed to helping each other succeed. Your female coworkers would be preoccupied with earning a living. They'd be helpful, considerate, and good-natured. They'd be there for the good of the company and for the good of enhancing your job. They'd put their individual goals on the backburner. Your female coworkers would support you when you take on a difficult task. Your female coworkers would comfort you when you need comforting. But most importantly, there'd be no hating.

In a perfect world, your female coworkers would support you. Instead, it's every woman for herself. Women hating on other women in the workplace has become so normal it's practically expected. Its women, not men, who are keeping each other from succeeding; who keep that glass ceiling intact. We should be working together in peace. We should be building each other up, not tearing each other down. None of this is benefiting women. In fact, it's doing anything but. While we're busy ruining each other at work, men are able to put 100% of their time and energy into their job and getting ahead. More men make it to top positions because they aren't sidetracked by hating on their male coworkers or being hated on by them. It should be us against them; instead it's us against each other. With all that women have, and continue to achieve and accomplish in the workplace, they shouldn't have to constantly watch their backs and worry about defending themselves from their fellow female coworkers. Women should be able to focus on their common goals in the workplace instead of focusing on destroying each other or protecting themselves from being destroyed.

As women in the workforce, we need to be there to support each other. Women need to be successful and grow. Women need to encourage other women for this to happen. Women need to coach, mentor, and provide moral support to other women. Women need to work together to help each other, not hate on each other. Women need to work well together. Together WE can tackle and do anything, whether it's to become President of the United States, to run a Fortune 500 company, or to be the next Oprah and influence the world. We need to dream big and dream together.

The future- is there one?

Is there a positive future for women in the workplace? Will the male to female workplace ratio revert to what it was 50 years ago? If women continue to force other women to quit or get them fired, the workplace will continue to be dominated by males. Everything we have worked so hard to achieve over the past several decades will have been for nothing. Yet, this is the path we head down if women continue hating on their fellow female coworkers. Women used to face the obstacle of entering the workforce; now they face the problem of staying in it.

As the future currently stands, women will continue to get fired or be forced to quit due to hating by their female coworkers. Administration will continue to look the other way. Coworkers will continue to not have each other's backs. Few women will be able to move up the career ladder if other women keep holding them back. Women will need to start putting aside 10% of their earnings for future "hating" that leaves them without a job. From where I sit there's NO positive future for women in the workplace. The only future women can expect is to get a job and *maybe* be able to stay there.

The future will only hold more violence. Push someone enough and they will react—and who could really blame them? They weren't protected and felt they had no other alternative or recourse. When you're desperate because you're losing your home, you're losing your health insurance, your family and friends don't understand, your emotional stability is shot, and you were already slightly on the edge, what is violence when you feel like you have nothing to live for? Then people will blame you when all you did was react to daily abuse. For every action, there is a reaction. With no laws, companies, employees, and lawmakers need to be prepared for an increase in work-related violence.

Proposed laws would require employers to step in and intervene in an effective manner and give targets the right to sue. Legal accountability is the only thing that will eliminate workplace hating. Without laws, hating will continue. Companies will continue to ignore, look the other way, and do nothing. The longer we go without policies or laws against workplace bullying and harassment, the worse the bullying and harassment becomes as haters become more skilled and know what they can get away with.

I'd like to say that the future of women in the workplace has a great outlook. I'd like to say that I believe that companies and lawmakers will put policies in place against this type of behavior. However, after the number of women I have spoken to that were so scarred they are now out on permanent leave, I can't in good conscience say I believe this. Their companies were willing to look the other way and I don't see that changing anytime soon. At least not until lawmakers, who don't seem to care, put laws in place.

Shana

I connected with Shana on Facebook. Her story instantly made me think of the page in my book that discusses reasons why people want to leave but can't. Shana had a felony charge and felt she had no choice but to stay where she was as she'd had difficulty in the past finding work. Unfortunately, her employer knew this.

Right off the bat she told me, "HR is there for the employer." Unfortunately, this was a phrase I would hear and read many times while doing research for this book. She worked in a restaurant with a cook who told her right away that she was bipolar. "She thought that by explaining her behavior away, it was forgivable. Being bipolar was a way to justify her behavior," Shana told me. She said the cook would get in her face and yell at her when the restaurant was short-staffed or too busy. Shana became her verbal punching bag, as they both worked in the kitchen together.

On the frequent trips the cook made to the dining room, she would curse at the waitresses in front of the customers. If that wasn't bad enough, she would even yell profanity at customers and tell them to leave.

Shana, who was otherwise happy at her job, decided to complain to management. Unfortunately, the owner was always busy and never there. No one from HR returned her calls. She quit several times but would always go back. Finally, she went on medicine to cope with her coworker and in an attempt to stay employed there.

Eventually, she did quit FOR GOOD and miraculously they didn't fight her unemployment. In fact, it was the total opposite — the owner called her several times and begged her to come back. He even offered to pay her off the books so she could still collect unemployment, but she refused.

Kylie

Kylie always considered herself fortunate in the business world. She loved her job, her boss, and her female coworkers. She was also fortunate enough to be happily married with four kids.

Her team at work was all female and consisted of someone just out of college, another newly engaged, and, finally, Gina, a woman who had been married for five years-thus, making Kylie the only one with children. Gina had been trying to conceive for several years. Unsuccessful, she became more and more bitter. She began to take out her anger on her female coworkers with children. If Kylie came in late due to a sick kid or left early for a school recital, Gina would give her the cold shoulder and extra work. She'd complain to anyone who would listen that Kylie put her kids first and that it was unfair that those without kids be punished. She attacked other females with children, but Kylie, being on her team, received the brunt of it. During Gina's first round of in vitro-fertilization, her anger increased as her hormones became out of whack. She spent half her time crying at her desk and the other half trying to get out of doing her work. The last straw was when Kylie took an unexpected day off due to her daughter's appendicitis. Gina "forgot" to relay the phone message to their boss. Eventually, Kylie took a pay cut and went somewhere else where she wouldn't have to put up with Gina and her issues.

Joelle

Like many of the women I interviewed, I connected with Joelle on Facebook. Joelle thinks she'll be in therapy for the rest of her life. She was diagnosed with anxiety, depression, and PTSD, due to abuse in the workplace. "People don't realize how bad it can be. Lives will never be the same. I don't know how these people go to sleep at night knowing how they destroyed someone's life. No one should have to go to work in fear. I now constantly look over my shoulder," she said. Joelle thinks a lot of haters hate because they are insecure about their jobs as there's little job security today. She thinks haters go after people who are well-liked, educated, accommodating, and those who do their job well.

Joelle was knowledgeable and had over 35 years of experience. She worked in a healthcare management center as the business office manager. She'd managed the startup of several ambulatory surgical centers. In 2010 another center opened closer to her home, so she asked for a transfer, which was granted. She was trained her first week there, by a woman who was then fired. This made Joelle unpopular. Joelle had no idea that someone would be fired and that she'd be her replacement. People became hostile towards her. One woman, a good friend of the woman who had been let go, was open in her dislike of Joelle. She would avoid speaking to her and would instead send up to 60 emails a day. Even if it was a quick question she could have easily asked her in person, it would be sent via email. Was she trying to create a paper trail? A hostile work environment? Or both? She wouldn't talk to her, but she would talk *about* her to everyone in the office as well as to the management companies (which acted as shareholders). New employees would be friendly to her at first, but once her hater took them under her wing they too would go out of their way to avoid her. Joelle had no idea what she was saying about her for people to treat her so poorly, but it was enough to put her over the edge. Even management had started to be less friendly to her.

Joelle was at the end of her rope. She had enough stress in her personal life and couldn't deal with it at work too. She was hospitalized for chest pains. Her doctor told her it was either she quit her job to lessen her stress or he'd see her back within the year with a heart attack. She quit her job with nothing lined up. She put in a claim for unemployment but was denied. Her credit was ruined and her house went into foreclosure; thankfully she was able to keep it. "Your hater will keep after you until she has achieved what she set out to do. You'll never be, emotionally or physically, the same person you were before it happened."

"Women are hating on their female coworkers, because they can and get away with it!"
-Heather L. Hodsden, "Women Who Hate Other Women"

Conclusion

More than ten years after my termination from Sayreville, I found myself sitting on the other side of the desk. An employee had reported to Human Resources (me) that she was being harassed and bullied by her coworkers, who of course were all female. She said there would be no issues until 6pm, when the manager went home, and then the behavior would start. They would boss her around, make her move to a different work station, and talk about her. As soon as she told me it didn't start until the manager left, I knew she was telling the truth. Her boss "assumed" she was the problem since it was happening with numerous females. Her boss wanted me to terminate her to get rid of the problem. I refused. There was no way this employee was going to lose her job on my watch. I told her boss that we didn't have a single write-up on the individual and that she claimed she was being bullied and harassed. I got the employee transferred and she was able to keep her job. I was able to save one person by transferring her to a different department and perhaps someday I will save someone else. But most stories don't have a happy ending.

During the recession I worked at a restaurant with a gentleman named Demetri (name not changed). It was obvious he didn't analyze the behavior of his coworkers. He didn't dwell on his coworkers' past issues or mistakes. When an issue arose, he dealt with it and moved on- issue solved and forgotten five minutes later. He dealt with facts and he confronted people who made mistakes. He took peoples' actions at face value and didn't analyze the "whys". Women need to work like this.

If you google "issues with bosses" you'll get almost five million hits. It's not considered uncommon to discuss how one's boss is out to get them or how someone left a job due to a boss. Now try googling "issues with coworkers". Fewer hits. Less talked about. More taboo. Now google "issues with female coworkers". Even fewer hits. Completely taboo. Not PC to discuss. Most consider it in your head and not a real problem. Yet, it exists. And until things are done to change it, it will continue to exist. Will this topic become less taboo to talk about in years to come? We can only hope so.

Call it hating, harassment, bullying, emotional abuse, mobbing, or anything else you want—it exists and can ruin your life or the life of someone you care about. Hating isn't limited to any specific kind of industry. No size or type of company is immune to it. Whether you're in a diner with twenty employees, at a school with several hundred, or at a global multi-international company with several thousand— you're not immune to it. It happens anywhere and everywhere.

In an ideal world, no one would have to go through this—everyone would be nice, companies would have policies against hating, and the United States would have laws against it. As of 2018, no states have passed the Healthy Workplace Bill. We are one of the last countries to not have anti-hating laws in place. We need to urge our legislators to enact laws against workplace hating just as we need to hold our employers accountable. Likewise, we need to sue our employer to show them we mean business when we're not heard.

When we attack and go after our own, we're only hurting our gender. I shouldn't have been able to write a book on this topic, because it shouldn't be happening. Unfortunately, hating is a reality for many women. Women are ruining other women's careers and lives. People need to know and understand this. We aren't paranoid, and we aren't making this up. This is real. Former targets of workplace hating can be affected for years to come- financially, physically, and emotionally. It can ruin your life. It can set you off course. It can derail your future plans and goals. If I'd gone back to Sayreville for one more year, I would have been able to buy a home. One recession and fifteen years later, it's still a dream I've never been able to accomplish.

Unfortunately, we don't live in an ideal world and we rarely work in an ideal workplace. Over the course of your career you'll encounter many difficult personalities in the workplace. You can pick your friends, but you can't pick your coworkers. Everyone comes to work with one form of baggage or another. Whether it's a preconceived notion, a past experience that still irks them, or a current situation at home- it doesn't give anyone the right to take it out on a fellow female coworker. At the end of the day, we are all professionals, no matter what. We need to remember that and act like it. We need to get work done and put on a professional front while doing so. If you feel that you cannot do so, then I suggest you go out on disability because WE DON'T WANT TO WORK WITH YOU.

Many women have no choice, but to leave their job or end up in the psych ward. There are many support groups (MAD, AA, Working Moms) out there, but where are the support groups for women who are being hated on and driven out of their jobs by their female coworkers? This epidemic exists and until steps are made to get rid of the problem it's not going to go away.

Unless you're a masochist, no one wants to spend day after day, year after year, in a work environment where they are constantly belittled, hated on, put down, talked about, screamed at, sabotaged, and harassed. Women shouldn't have to worry about other women spreading rumors about them and trying to get them fired. It's unfortunate that your coworkers have the power to make your work life miserable. It's even more unfortunate that a miserable work life can affect your home life, your family, your relationships, your health, and more. People have enough to worry about — taking care of someone sick, parents, spouse/ partner, health, house, kids, finances, and sending kids to college. People have enough problems and stress in their life without their female coworkers creating drama where there is none.

Most of us don't go to work for fun. Most people need to work for a living. We go because we have to earn money. Anyone who sabotages another person's livelihood deserves what they get. It doesn't matter what's going on in your female coworker's personal life. It doesn't matter what's going on in your female coworker's professional life. There is no excuse for her to take it out on you.

Don't ever let another person (male or female) make you doubt your ability to keep a job. Most likely, these are people who have never been sabotaged at a job. People who have never been the object of resentment or jealousy at work. People who have never been viciously or angrily attacked for no reason. Let's face it — if it hadn't happened to you, someone close to you, or you hadn't seen it happen, would you believe it? Some of these stories are almost too outlandish to be true. Plus, it's easier to blame the target: "Oh, maybe she wasn't doing a good job" OR "maybe she has problems getting along with others" OR how about "it's her own fault — these things always happen to her".

I'd love to tell you that I made up the stories in this book. But I didn't. I'd love to tell you that I've never experienced or witnessed females hating, harassing, bullying, and sabotaging other females in the workplace. But I have. I'd love to tell you that I've never seen females forcing other females to quit or getting them fired. But I have first-hand experience with the latter. I'd love to tell you that this book is a figment of my imagination and that the issue of women hating on other women in the workplace doesn't exist and isn't true. But that would be a lie. Having heard all these tales of hating in the workplace has made me angry. It's not fair that the majority of these haters still have their jobs and we were fired or were forced to resign. While we have lost our jobs most of our haters have lost nothing.

As for the impact my experience has had on me? I don't trust my female coworkers. I try to avoid them. The less I interact with them the better. I often question their good intentions due to my experience. I'm suspicious and do not easily trust others. Not only am I suspicious and careful with women at work, but it's also carried into my personal life. I'm always on guard. If it seems too good to be true it probably is.

If you're the victim of hating speak up. It's easier to do nothing and just quit. But if she's done this to you, I can almost guarantee you're not the first, nor will you be the last. People I've spoken with regret not telling people why they left and what went on. By doing nothing the problem won't go away. By leaving you've only solved your problem, not the problem as a whole, and you have not discouraged the person from continuing on with her hating.

If you know you're on your way to being fired, COMPLAIN. They've already made up their mind to get rid of you. "Harass" management with your complaints. Don't leave quietly. They get annoyed? So what—you're likely on your way out anyway. It's not your fault if management is incompetent and not doing their job. **Complain, complain, and complain.** Then complain some more. Companies won't put policies in place until they need to. Go public. Sue them. Hit them where it hurts. Companies should be financially responsible to targets. They need to be held accountable for their actions, or lack thereof. More employees need to sue their employers until they take action and put a system in place that will remove hating from the workplace.

If hating has happened to you, please know that you're not alone. Don't be ashamed. Don't keep quiet. Tell your story. Share it with others. You may be surprised- the person you choose to share your story with may have one of their own to share too.

If you know someone being hated on, the best thing you can do is be a friend. Be there for them. Lend an ear. Give them sympathy and a shoulder to cry on. Show them empathy and compassion. Reassure them that it's not their fault. Let them know they have options. Most importantly, make sure they document everything. You may not feel like you're doing much, but just letting the person know you're there for them and in their corner will mean the world to them. And share this book with them.

Hating occurs because it's allowed to happen. It happens every day, everywhere, most specifically in the United States, because there's no law against it.
Going to work in a peaceful environment shouldn't be a dream—it should be a reality. Please write to your local Congress to urge them to pass an anti-bullying in the workplace law.

"Women will never break through the glass ceiling if they're always looking for a shard to stab each other in the back."

-Cristal Carrington, *Dynasty*

Useful websites

www.shrm.org

www.eeoc.gov/

www.dol.gov/

www.ada.gov/

www.osha.gov/

www.nela.org

www.workplacebullying.org/

www.ourbullypulpit.com/

workplacebullyingadvisors.com/

abusergoestowork.com/

http://inhumaneresources.wix.com/workplacebullying

www.thepetitionsite.com/1/protect-us-workers/

www.takethebullybythehorns.com

www.bullyfreeworld.com

www.bullying.co.uk

www.bullybeware.com

www.bullybusters.org

http://www.bullyfreeatwork.com/

http://ratemycompanyusa.com/news/

www.bullywhisperer.com

http://www.stopthatnow.org/

http://www.stopworkplacebullies.com/

https://stopworkplacebullies.wordpress.com/

http://www.workplacebullyingcoalition.org/

http://www.stopemployerbullying.org/pages/home.shtml

https://www.causes.com/causes/199891-stop-work-place-bullying-mobbing

http://www.bulliesandenergyvampires.com.au/

https://newworkplace.wordpress.com/

http://thebullyexposed.com/
www.workdoctor.com
https://en.wikipedia.org/wiki/Workplace_bullying
www.bullyonline.org
www.bullyoffline.org
http://www.nyhwa.org/
bullyfreeworkplace.org

References

Adams, Scott. (1998). *The Joy of Work*. New York. Harper Business.

Apter, PhD., Terri & Josselon, PhD., Ruthellen. (1998). *Best Friends: The Pleasures and Perils of Girls' & Women's Friendships*. New York. Crown Publishers.

Babiak, Paul and Hare, Robert D. (2009). *Snakes in Suits: When Psychopaths go to Work*. Harper Business.

Barnes, JD., Patricia. (2012). *Surviving Bullies, QueenBees, and Psychopaths in the Workplace*.

Benjamin, Susan. (2008). *Perfect Phrases for Dealing with Difficult People*. McGraw-Hill

Briles, Dr. Judith. (1999). *Women to Women 2000*. Far Hills, NJ. New Horizon Press.

Cavaiola, Alan & Lavender, Neil. *Toxic Coworkers: How to Deal with Dysfunctional People on the Job*.

Chesler, Phyllis. (2001). *Woman's Inhumanity to Woman*. New York. Thunder's Mouth Press/Nation Books.

Cronin, Lynn and Fine, Howard. (2010). *Damned if She Does, Damned if She Doesn't*. Amherst, New York. Prometheus Books.

Crowe, Sandra. (1999). *Since Strangling Isn't an Option*. Berkley Publishing Group.

Crowley, Katherine & Elster, Kathi. (2013). *Mean Girls at Work*. McGraw Hill

Crowley, Katherine & Elster, Kathi. (2006). *Working with You is Killing Me*. New York. Warner Business Books

Davenport, Phd., Noa, & Disler Schwartz, Ruth & Pursell Elliott, Gail. (1999*). Mobbing: Emotional Abuse in the American Workplace*. IOWA. Civil Society Publishing

Demarais, Phd., Ann & White, Phd., Valerie. (2004). *First Impressions: What you don't know about how others see you.* Bantam Books

DiMarco, Haley. (2005). *Mean Girls All Grown Up: Surviving Catty and Conniving Women.*

Pinkos Cobb, Ellen. (June 24, 2014). *Workplace Bullying Protections Differ Globally*

Evans, Gail. (May 2003). *She Wins, You Win.* New York. Gotham Books

Gurwitch, Annabelle. (2006). *Fired.* New York. Simon & Schuster

Heim, Pat PhD & Murphy, PhD. Susan. (2001). *In the Company of Women: Turning Workplace Conflict into Powerful Alliances.* New York. Tarcher/Putnam.

Hirigoyen, Marie-France. (2004). *Stalking the Soul: Emotional Abuse and the Erosion of Identity.* New York. Helen Marx Books.

Huppke, R. W. (2013, July 7). Harassed at work? Suing is now harder. The Baltimore Sun. Business and Jobs section, p. 4.

Horn, Sam. (2002). *Take the Bully by the Horns.* New York. St. Martin's Griffin.

Jansen, Julie. (2006). *You Want Me to Work with Who? Eleven Keys to a Stress-Free, Satisfying, and Successful Work-Life.* New York. Penguin Books

Kohut, Margaret. (2008). *The Complete Guide to Understanding, Controlling, and Stopping Bullies and Bullying at Work.* Florida. Atlantic Publishing Group.

Madden, Tara Roth. (1987). *Women vs. Women: The Uncivil Business War.* Amacon Books.

Maltby, Lewis. (2009). *Can They Do That?* New York. Penguin.

Mattice, Catherine & Sebastian, E.G. (2012). *Back Off! Your Kick-Ass Guide to Ending Bullying at Work.* Pennsylvania. Infinity Publishing.

Mooney, Nan. (2005). *I Can't Believe She Did That.* New York. St. Martin's Griffin.

Namie, PhD., Gary & Namie, PhD., Ruth. (2009). *The Bully at Work: What you can do to stop the hurt and Reclaim your Dignity on the Job.*

Needham, Andrea. (2003). *Workplace Bullying.* New Zealand. Penguin Books.

Reardon, PhD. Kathleen Kelley. (2005). *It's All Politics.* New York. Doubleday

Rex W. Huppke. (Sunday 7/7/13). *Harassed at Work? Suing is now harder.* Baltimore Sun Pg. 4.

Sanborn, Claudia. (2015). The Yellow "Sick" Road: A Nurse's Travels for 22 Years".

Shapiro Barash, Susan. (2006). *Tripping the Prom Queen.* New York. St. Martin's Press. Sheppard, Roy & Cleary, Mary. (2007). *That Bitch: Protect Yourself against Women with Malicious Intent. England.* Centre Publishing.

Simmons, Rachel. (2011). *Odd Girl Out.* First Mariner Books.

Solomon, Muriel. (1990). *Working with Difficult People.* Prentice Hall, Simon Schuster.

Spindel, Patricia. (2008). *Psychological Warfare at Work.*

Sutton PHD, Robert. (2010). *The No Asshole Rule: Building a Civilized Workplace and surviving one that isn't.* Business Plus. Hachette Brook Group.

Tanenbaum, Leora. (2002). *Catfight: Women and Competition.* New York. Seven Stories Press

Warstad, Jonas. (2014). *The Bully Exposed.* California

http://www.allure.com/beauty-trends/how-to/2007/How_To_Confront_A_Coworker

www.workplacebullying.org/2011/05/16/wow

http://www.shrm.org/hrdisciplines/employeerelations/articles/pages/whybulliesthriveatwork.aspx

www.shrm.org/hrdisciplines/global/articles/pages/us-drug-testing-rules.aspx

www.women.ezinemark.com/women-sabotage-and-bullying-oh-her-4f4764b62a8.html

www.sciencedaily.com/releases/2011/10/111006133020.htm

http://www.washingtonpost.com/national/health-science/is-your-boss-making-you-sick/2014/10/20/60cd5d44-2953-11e4-8593-da634b334390_story.html

http://www.nytimes.com/2009/05/10/business/10women.html?pagewanted=all&_r=0

www.nbcnews.com/id/38060072/ns/business-careers/

http://www.shrm.org/hrdisciplines/global/articles/pages/workplace-bullying-protections-differ-globally.aspx

www.nbcnews.com/id/38060072/ns/business-careers/

http://www.shrm.org/legalissues/employmentlawareas/pages/workplace-bullying.aspx

www.businessmanagementdaily.com/39551/you-can-handle-an-office-bully?

http://www.thegrindstone.com/2011/05/16/work-life-balance/women-on-women-bullying-in-the-workplace-on-the-rise/

https://www.shrm.org/resourcesandtools/hr-topics/risk-management/pages/workplace-bullying-laws.aspx

http://lawprofessors.typepad.com/adjunctprofs/2009/06/not-all-bullies-are-men.html

Acknowledgements

I wrote most of the acknowledgements in 2010. Even though they may not necessarily reflect the place certain people have in my life today, I wanted to keep it as it was.

I want to start by thanking God, as one of my favorite writers Kimberla Lawson Roby always does. Thank you, Lord, for making me the person I am. Though my life has been more difficult than not, I am one of the most educated and well-read people I know. Thank you for giving me the ability to write this book — not an easy feat. I was exposed to reading and books at an early age, thanks to my family. My Mom always read to me as a child. One of my first set of books was given to me by my Great Uncle when I was 5. It was a fabulous set of McGuffey's Eclectric Readers. My Great Uncle and Grandmother Hodsden then introduced me to *Nancy Drew*, when I was 7. I continued to read at an advanced level and was reading my Grandmother Miller's V.C. Andrews books when I was 9. I continued to read voraciously and read my first Stephen King novel at age 14. A book is so much more than a book — a book is a friend.

A special thanks to all the people who shared their hating stories with me, especially all those on the Facebook group pages. We shouldn't have to go through this to be employed. We can hold our head up high knowing that we are better than our haters.

Angie Ecklund- To my other half, thank you for always believing in me and especially in this project. What can I say? You're my anchor and my support. Where would I be without you? May we continue to have better adventures and memories than everyone else. California and Europe await us.

Allen Kalik aka Louis/lui- Thanks for always being there for me and listening to my "work issues". Sorry you never got to read my book. I miss you. Not a day goes by that I don't think about you and how you influenced my life. You were a GREAT friend. You'll always have a special place in my heart. Xoxo Louise aka Bruyère

Jimmy McPherson aka Zephyr- Merci for the suggestion to get a hobby. May someone **literally** always be there to pull me out of quicksand when I'm sinking. Fondly, *AND GUEST*

To all my TKE (Tau Kappa Epsilon) fraternity brothers that I've partied with over the years- from DC, to Long Beach, CA to NYC, to numerous TKE houses in NJ to the "TKE" slumber parties @my dorm room: Furley, Cel, Cruz, Kyle, Dan, Bob, Jon, Ben, Wes, Brian, Kenny, Tommy, Michael, Wayne, my "little" Nikita, Kevin, Jeff, Rafael, Frankie, Nader, Greg, Jay, Neal, Darren, Steve, Joe, Joey P., Mike, Pat, Eric, Nick, Nigel, Alex, Sean (Mary Margaret Candy ASS!). To all my Kean College brothers: THANK YOU FOR LETTING ME BE YOUR SWEETHEART!!!!!!!! YITB PEACE APPLE...!

To Allan P Hanson Jr III Esquire Ghost, Rich Hsiung, & Sandip Mukherjee, three of my favorite TKEs and exes- my everlasting love. Thank you for your support and for always being there for me when I needed you.

Michele Lester- Thank you for helping me get on the plane. May we someday both end up in Europe at the same time.

Gram Cowell- My favorite socialist, we'll always have Paris.

Kelly Doan- Thank you for always being your usual positive and optimistic self. ☺

A tous mes profs et camarades de classe de Middlebury - Anyone want to try translating this book into French? Quelqu'un voudrait-il essayer de traduire ce livre en français? ☺ Merci pour cette expérience. J'ai passé le quatre meilleurs étés de ma vie avec vous. Surtout à tous les profs: Elise, Monsieur France, Monsieur Agostini, Monsieur Sala, Monsieur Fonkoua, Didier, Bachir, Badreddine, Christophe, Monsieur et Madame Motron, Monsieur Redonnet, Monsieur Bure, Monsieur et Madame Hontanx, Madame Batts, Madame Baccar, Madadme Bertolini, Monsieur et Madame Noiray. Vous êtes tous fabuleux. Je ne vous oublierai jamais et les moments qu'on a vécu ensemble. Vous me manquez beaucoup.

Tony D'Orazio- Thank you for your love, support, and guidance.

Sherri Wisk Vernaci- Thank you for always being supportive and being there for me. Blondes rule!

Jim Roache- My writing mentor. I picked up a pen and first started writing at the age of 13 thanks to you. Thanks for being a good phone friend. PS. LOSER!

Brian Caughie- Thank you for EVERYTHING.

Mom- Thank you for your editing and everything in between. I'm such a well-read person because of you. Xo ☺

Lola#bestie- Disney? And, yes, you need to fly. Next book is for you ☺ XO

Baby A- I'm so proud to be your AuntMom! Start packing your bags- France here we come. PS- I owe you a brownie @Chocolate Face

Lauren, Colin, Alexis, & Lindsay- My pride and joy. I couldn't love you any more than if I'd given birth to you myself. PS. Avalon bagel next time I'm in town.

To DW, CD, AA, and VM- Your job experiences gave me lots of material and great stories to share. Sorry you had to go through all this. ☹

To all the wonderful professionals I got to virtually connect with while studying for my GBA certification-it was a pleasure: Paul Lench, Lauren Howell, Janel Poster, Tracy Anderson, Richard Bartlett, Rose Burke, Suzanne Bavier, Christina Lawton, Jeannine Herrera, Beth Levy, Mary Ann Till, Rachell Bowers, LaTonia McCane, Nicole Perez-Wiker, Wardah Porter, Michelle Mills, Sharie Hyder, Nina Atchanah, and Tami Moore.

To all my fellow socialists and/or liberal friends: Uncle Skipper, Bugzy, Lola, Steven, Cruz, Cindy, Erika, Sean (STA), Kelly, Gram, Wayne, Ann, Alex, Gheorge, Lori, Allen (RIP), Victor, Joachim, David, Clay, Harry, Marty, Karl, Da'Shauna, Ned, Paul, Michele, Adrienne, Gerson, Johnny, Angie, Rick, Joe (RIP), Annie, Andrew, Dominic, Elizabeth, Chad, Randy, Donald, Brendan, Lyonel, Sam, Bruno, Joey, Shawna, Helen, Rachel, Jim R., Tony, Jimmy H., Tracy, Lisa, Jackie, Monte, AK, HW, AS, SJ, BC, AT, LH, TL, RM, PR, MC, BRUCE, and most of my other friends- may we someday become more aligned to the European system of doing things. May we someday live in a world where education and healthcare are free, and capitalism no longer rules, and people are free to love whomever they want.

Joanna Kirvin aka the President- Whom I never would have met if we both weren't unemployed together. You're one of the strongest women I have ever met. I know life is hard at times. Hold your head up high. You're a beautiful person. PS. BURBERRY RULES!

To some of the most beautiful inside and out, confident, successful, and strong women I have met in my life: (Note maiden names used) Barbara Ann Flacco, Christyne Danysh, Lane McKenna, Jennifer Schoenleber, Christie Micsko, Diana Franklin, Erika Andrews, Cathleen Jennings, Viana DeAndrade, Andrea Scaramelli, Vanessa Antkiw, Lori Fournier, Amy Larsen, Desirée Moses, Adrianna Mackeown, Maribeth Freeman, and Raquel Alvarado- you're all so fabulous- don't let anyone ever tell you differently!

To my favorite upper eastsider Nick Koutsoulidakis- Maybe one of my next books will be about you. ☺

To the ones I loved and lost- BHH, NM, BM, and especially AHE (whom hurt me numerous times and worse than anybody else)- YOUR LOSS!

In 2012, I picked up and moved to Maryland for a better life. I had only been there once and that was to find an apartment. One month later I moved, not knowing a soul. To the wonderful friends I made and great people I encountered during the time I lived in Ellicott City, Maryland: My wonderful neighbor Carol, my scrapbooking friend Sandi, former coworkers @NP- Edie, Tal, Gabe, Donna, Desirée, and Debra. My gym buddies- Andrew, Allie, and Dominic. My meetup friends- Lisa, Mandy, Kristin, Kristine, Ann, and Wayne. My CHRA (Baltimore County Human Resources Chapter) pals- Page, Phil, Ryan, and of course, Bernie. And everyone else- Whitney, Angie C., Maurice, Renaud, Chuck, and Agi. Thank you to all the wonderful warm people who helped my transition there.

Helen Kopeck-Domingo- My former boss, mentor, fellow vegan, feminist, and liberal- thank you for giving me a chance in the Human Resources world.

Keith Capps- My former coworker and workplace bestie. The nicest coworker I ever had! It was an honor sitting next to you. Thank you for always having my back. You'll always be my favorite cubicle mate.

To the Howard County, Maryland SHRM (Society of Human Resources) Chapter- I loved being a part of your group and miss our meetings. Thank you for everything.

Thank you to everyone at Starbucks, Panera Bread, Caffe Benne, and Tropical Smoothie in Columbia and Ellicott City, Maryland who served me while I spent dozens of hours researching and writing this book.

To all my Freehold Twp. students- What can I say? The first year is always a trial: Nancy, Dan and the bee, Dana, Fran, Pinar, Danielle, Shari, Stéphanie, salut les filles (Kristin, Jessica, Ashley), Anne, Jennie, Ajay, Francois, the Kellys, Mike, Stéphanie, Diana, Mohammed et son calendrier, and last but not least Robert.

To all my former Sayreville students- It was an honor teaching you and learning from you. It was a pleasure spending two years with you. I hope you all someday make it to France. Bai & John (Monsieur les yeux qui bougent), Courtney, Amanda, Eunice, Jethro, Tim, Felipe, Priya, Sara, Taras, Sylwia, Natalia, Jen, Jenny, Jennifer, Smita, Paul, Matt, Christie, Ingrid, Mawulom, Marissa, Candice, Nataliya, Christina, Kriston, Gary, Dafina, Kesha, Lydia, Neil,

Demetrio, Tina, Jackie, Rochelle, Kateryna, Sammy, Agatha, Alejandra, Rênée, Aubrey, Lindsey, Asel, Nicole, Arnold, John S., Aimée, Vivian C., Valeriya, Ellen, Jane, Sadé, Wrighton, Keith, Omotola, Jamie, Gabrielle, Dominique, Hinal, Joyce, Stéphanie (RIP), Keisha (RIP), Dan, Karese, Beverly, Leon, Stefanie, Dupé, Nancy, Kirby, Rafael, Vida, Imani, Jess, Anthony, Jonah, Abigail, Liz, Angie, Nada, Joshua, Jessica, Agnes, Julia, Heather, Shauntele', Morgan, Michelle, Daniela, ma "fille" Kristine et sa BFF Vivian, Rachel (Gilmore Girls rules), Hans, and of course Clément. And the ones that I failed that still loved me anyway: Avril, Josh, Brian, Trevor, Charles, and Judy. PS. Allons enfants de la patrie…

Chronic Fatigue Syndrome

While I have your ear, I'd like to talk about another cause that is close to my heart- Chronic Fatigue Syndrome. There is little known about it, as little research has been done. Instead, millions of people are losing their life to this. People, who if cured, could have been the scientist to cure cancer, the next President of the US, or the next person to climb Mount Everest. Most people aren't lucky enough to rebound from chronic fatigue syndrome.

Like many, I never fully understood this illness or how debilitating it could be. Chronic fatigue syndrome is a serious health condition. It can be caused by something else, as it was for me, or occur for an unknown reason. Chronic fatigue is a crippling life altering disease that reduces quality of life. It's an isolating illness that has had a profound effect on my life.

Chronic fatigue affects over 1 million people just in the United States. Less than 20% are able to hold full-time jobs. Many go on permanent disability. Chronic fatigue syndrome can take a fully functioning person, as it did me, and make them housebound. CFS can last for many years. Unfortunately, for most it lasts a lifetime.

In December 2012, I moved from New Jersey to Maryland for work. I'd spent the prior 5 1/2 years, during the recession, unemployed. During that time, I'd lost my apartment and had to move back in with my Mom, which was hours away from where I'd lived most of my life. By moving, I'd lost my life and my friends--it was horrible to say the least. Those years were very bleak, depressing, humiliating, and degrading. Within ONE week of moving to Maryland, I had a FT job with benefits. Wonderful, wasn't it?

Within 6 weeks of moving to Ellicott City, Maryland, I felt exhausted. I ignored it in the beginning. After all, I was happy. If I hadn't been through everything I had been through unemployment wise, I would've probably left. But I liked my apartment. I liked that there was less traffic than in North Jersey. Everyone there was friendlier than the people in the NYC area. It was easy to get a job. I was on HR committees and networking. I was happier than I'd been in years. There was no real reason to leave, except I was tired.

Whenever I'd return to NJ for the weekend, I'd feel better. But then upon my return to Maryland I'd be more exhausted than ever. Not tired, but exhausted. Yes, there's a very big difference. You might be tired if you stay up late one night, but you can still have energy and "push" through. Someone with CFS wakes up (if they were even able to sleep) with no energy. They are already depleted and in the negative when they start their day. No matter how many hours of sleep I got, 7 to 13, I'd still have the same level of exhaustion. Often, I'd wake up more tired than I'd been when I went to sleep.

So, in order to live out my day I'd have to constantly ignore what my body was telling me. I'd have to ignore the weirdness I felt, the brain fog, the fatigue, and how I just didn't feel right. I continued to push myself to do things even though I barely enjoyed them. To be honest with you, I was too sick to know what was going on in my own body, much less what was going on around me. I was constantly in a daze for everything I did. And what I did do was done in a dream like state.

My health continued to decline. I started to experience memory issues and every time I'd brush my teeth; my enamel would fall off. I became unable to sleep late on my days off and would wake up numerous times during the night.

Eventually, I had bloodwork done and my neutrophils were elevated, which was a concern. My bloodwork also showed that my liver had gone down, but I was still in normal range. In addition, I was having horrible asthma problems. At first, I thought I thought it was because my downstairs neighbor was smoking cigarettes and marijuana. However, my problems continued after his departure. I've had asthma since 1994, but I'd never had to go to the ER for it until this point. I'd have to go to urgent care to get put on a nebulizer, which would help, but not for long. My breathing would worsen once I walked out of the Doctor's office and out into the "fresh" air.

Meanwhile, I saw a rheumatologist who tested me for the RA factor, as my Mother has RA, but it was negative. I continued to feel worse. I'd feel dizzy standing long periods of time, my body started to feel hot and achy, and I felt like the lights were shut off in my head.

Most days I could barely drive. I'd get into my car in the morning and just pray as I rolled on. I'd feel like I was going to black out. I'd be in a daze, clutching the wheel and literally clinching my hands to try and stay alert and avert the blackout feeling I had. This only caused me to get nervous, which in turn only made me feel worse. Yet I had no choice- I had to go to work. I'm sure I got behind the wheel hundreds of times when I shouldn't have. Subsequently, I've read that someone with CFS has a slower reaction time than someone legally intoxicated-not hard for me to believe!

My symptoms would worsen every time I left in the morning to go to work — although I didn't realize it at the time. The second I left the house and walked outside, I'd feel even more tired. My head also felt weird, but I didn't give it any thought. I figured I was maybe just stressed about work. If it was raining, I'd get a headache the second I walked outside. If I was very lucky, I wouldn't start coughing or have an asthma attack.

A little after a year there, I noticed that I was unable to get air into my nose. I thought it was a fluke. A month later, I realized it was still happening. I went on Afrin and suddenly I had energy again and felt so much better. Then I went on Dymista and for the first week it was a miracle- I felt great- like my normal New Jersey self. Unfortunately, after a week my tired Maryland self-returned. A cat scan determined that I needed sinus surgery.

I had surgery and was able to get up a little more air in my right side, but my left was still clogged almost 100%. I started to have a few allergy symptoms. I had runny eyes and a cough- this was the first and only time I ever had typical allergy symptoms. For some reason, whether it be walking outside my home or driving through trees, when exposed to my allergens I became exhausted. How I would have given anything to have been like everyone else who coughed, sneezed, and had a runny nose. I was allergy tested and allergic to almost 30 things. I'd been allergy tested 20 years prior but had tested negative. I was told that it was common to move to Maryland, "where there was always something blooming 24/7" and get allergies. I started allergy shots. In the beginning I'd have a little more energy on the days after I got my shot. While the allergy shots helped my asthma, they did nothing for my allergies. I'd often have reactions to the shots and have to backtrack. I continued to get worse, due to the double dose of allergens I was getting- from the shot and outside. This caused my eyelids to become swollen. You could literally see the inflammation when you looked at me. Originally, I thought that everyone who had allergies felt this bad. But apparently that isn't the case at all.

By this point my health was so bad that in November 2014, I was no longer able to hold down a FT job. My body aches were nonstop. My head felt congested 24/7. I felt like I had the flu. My sleep was constantly interrupted and even though I was exhausted I'd have insomnia and trouble sleeping. By this time, I was waking up 10 times a night, getting around 2-3 hours of sleep a night.

And what's worse is the worse I felt, the more disturbed my sleep would be that night. Now, where is the logic in that? You think that the more tired someone is, the better they can sleep, but oh no- not with chronic fatigue syndrome. The more tired you are, the more out of whack your body is, the more times you will wake up that night and be unable to sleep. It's a never-ending pattern. And sure, you may be able to fall back to sleep after waking up, but you'll be up at least 10 times during your eight hours of sleep. I'd say 8, but most people with CFS aren't lucky enough to get 8 hours of sleep.

My symptoms, which are typical of most CFS patients:
- sensitivity to light

- body aches
- dizziness/vertigo
- feelings of getting ready to black out
- asthma attacks
- profound fatigue
- headaches
- sinus pressure
- tenderness in my face
- earaches
- exhaustion
- no amount of sleep helps
- wake up feeling tired- often more tired than when you went to bed
- poor concentration
- low energy
- irritability
- sore throat
- mental fatigue

It became difficult for me to get through the day and do the things I needed to do each day. Unfortunately, I lived alone, in this state, where I knew not many and most on the superficial level, so I had only myself to depend on. Doing menial chores like going to the food store were often hard by now as sometimes I'd feel like I was going to black out when the allergies were bad out. When I couldn't avoid stores, I'd hold onto a shopping cart to stand and often have to crouch down and sit on the floor by the time I got up to the cashier. I once sat crouched on the ground in line at ShopRite for 20 minutes. I had no choice-the store was a nightmare and I had my birthday cake, which needed to be paid for. Often, I'd barely be able to get through the store, and then the line would be too long. All too often, I'd have to abandon my cart and go back and try again the following day. If I were somewhere where there wasn't a car and had to stand in line for a while, I'd have to lean on something. If there was nothing to lean on, I'd give up and leave. I never got to the point where I collapsed, but I did tremor. I was also wearing sunglasses in stores, as I'd developed a light sensitivity and the light in most stores was too bright for me.

Around this time, it was noted that my blood pressure and pulse were elevated. My sitting pulse was, and often still is 110. I've gotten some odd readings since I've been ill: 116/89 pulse 111, 105/84 pulse 104, and even 132/130 pulse 71. My blood pressure goes to a practically normal level in the summer but gets super high in the winter. I believe at this point I also had fibromyalgia and adrenal fatigue. Caffeine only made me more tired. I could drink a bottle of Pepsi before bed and fall asleep 10 minutes later. My system just wasn't right. I could never have done that when I was healthy. Instead I have a tired battered body with a heart rate of 110 resting, swollen eyes, and too many other symptoms to name.

I tried acupuncture, which did seem to help, but once I walked outside I'd once again feel exhausted and full of brain fog. I felt like my body was lacking something. I felt like I needed an injection of something my body didn't have enough of. The only question was what.

I lost years of my life to this. I was an active person before I became housebound with no social life. I was a 37-year-old, healthy, type A personality. I was a motivated individual who always wanted to take on more and more projects and tasks and volunteer, not just to be on a committee, but to be the head of the committee. I became someone who would just sleep through the day and do the bare minimum. I'd attempt to do more, but it would not always go so well. Reading and studying for the online class I was taking? Sure, if reading things five times over counted. Because that's exactly how many times I'd need to mentally absorb the material.

I was in the prime years of my life when I should be going out doing things, having fun, socializing, seeing friends, and going on vacations. Instead, I got little joy out of doing anything in life. It was more torture to get myself out of the house and doing something. When I pushed myself to be social, I never enjoyed it. It was more pain than gain. I'd be wasting energy, I should have saved for something I needed to do, on something I would get little pleasure out of.

I missed spending time with family and friends. Many had offered to go out to lunch with me or do things that we'd done prior to my illness. I felt like they didn't understand or perhaps couldn't grasp the concept of my illness. If I was well enough to do everything I'd been doing before I was sick, well then, I wouldn't be sick. What I needed were phone calls to cheer me up, texts asking how I was, already-prepared food for the days I was too ill to cook, and of course visits. I wanted people to take the time out of their busy schedules and lives (oh how I missed having one) to visit little old me.

I missed society and civilization, so any interactions brought me great joy. Instead what I got were just texts sparingly stating to contact them when I felt well enough to hang out. Well, what if I never felt well enough again?

Hadn't that ever crossed their minds? Cause it sure as hell had crossed mine- at least a dozen times a day and that was on a good day.

You find out who your friends are when you have something bad happen to you. Unfortunately, I could count mine on one hand. Most people are hypocrites and leave you in your darkest hour. CFS cost me a handful of friends. They either didn't understand or got tired of hearing about my health problems. I had more than one friend, tell me that I *"had too many problems even though they weren't my fault."* People didn't understand, especially because to them I looked fine. They think "this person must be ok, therefore it's in their mind". I was surrounded by friends who didn't really understand when I told them I was tired and had chronic fatigue. They'd just stare at me. Comments like "I'm tired too", OR "Why don't you take a nap", are stupid and meaningless to someone with this illness. Let them be in my body for a day and my mind- yes not to mention my mind which operates on the slowest pace of slow. I had thoughts I wanted to express and words I wanted to form and get out, but I was too tired to express myself intelligently. Eventually, I stopped reaching out to people, which is common. No one understood what I was going through. I grew tired of explaining it to people who didn't understand.

We live in a society where we donate old clothes and toys to hurricane victims, people that have lost their home in a fire, and other people who have suffered. Which is <u>great</u>, but what about the people that we actually KNOW that are down and out on their luck? What do we actually do for them? Why do we do more for people we don't know as opposed to the ones that we do? Is it because we can still distance ourselves from the situation as our involvement "ends" after we drop off our left-over worldly goods?

I missed work. I was angry I couldn't leave my home. Angry I had to turn down social invitations. Angry I didn't feel well enough to go shopping or do yoga. I had no life and was basically chained to my home. On many days all I could do was watch TV and knit. Often, I wasn't even well enough to do the latter. There were days when I could barely dress myself and absorb the simplest TV show.

I blamed myself. I knew I didn't feel correct, but I stayed in Maryland. I stayed there, because it was better than the alternative- returning to NJ to be unemployed. I was applying to jobs in NJ and NYC constantly while there, but to no avail. I think another reason I stayed was because I felt so sick I could barely even think anymore. Maybe if I had focused more on how I USED to feel- I'd have remembered and known something was so incredibly wrong with my system.

Towards the end of my stay in Maryland, I was no longer able to go to stores, the gym, or even get my allergy shot. By the time I ended up leaving Maryland for good, I could barely pack to my belongings and almost lost them, because I was too ill to pack them. Things were poorly packed, with high probability of breaking. God bless my understanding movers, because I was literally laying on the floor while my movers moved my belongings out.

So, I returned to NJ where I slept for 16 hours a day for several weeks. Sleep was still interrupted, lasting from 7pm until around 11am the following day. I started to get better on my own, but I still have brain fog, sleeping issues, and continue to react to allergens. Even during the winter, I can feel that my head is congested. Subsequent bloodwork showed that my B12 was very high and I was Vitamin D deficient. I also developed a sensitivity to gluten and soy. While my symptoms continue to get better, every time the southwest wind comes from the MD, area I feel like I'm back there.

I don't understand why there aren't more tests or protocol for what has happened to me. As of 2018 there is no blood test to measure CFS. This illness has been neglected and little research has been done on it. One reason is that our group has no voice. Most people with this are too sick to protest and be heard. Many are unable to get out of bed or sit up.

I don't understand why my body couldn't adjust to Maryland a.k.a. my new environment. I've only ever met 2 other individuals that have moved to Maryland and gotten ill like me. So, what exactly is going on in Maryland that is making people so ill they can barely function and get out of bed? My periodontist explained to me that Maryland is a very high inflammation area. In addition to the enamel falling off my teeth, I also had inflammation in my gum. My rosacea on my face, another sign of inflammation, was also very bad.

I don't know what is wrong with me or why it's so hard for someone to figure out. Why didn't the doctors in Maryland run more test on me? I don't understand why there wasn't a cure or why the allergy shots didn't work. I don't understand why allergies made me so sick. No one understands how exhausted and tired I've felt, because they simply just cough or blow their nose when they are exposed to allergies. I don't understand what my immune system is lacking. I don't know if I am on my way to developing an auto-immune disease. I was completely healthy in NJ until I moved to MD. I don't know if I will ever be 100% my former self or if this is how I will feel for the rest of my life. But after having researched CFS, I see that I'm one of the luckier ones- only 10% ever improve. I'm glad I'm in that 10%.

Heather L. Hodsden grew up in Cape May County, New Jersey. She has spent the majority of her life in North Jersey, minus the recession, where she lived in Howard County, Maryland.

Former high school French teacher, turned Human Resources professional, "Women Who Hate Other Women" is her first literary work. She coined the term "hating", which refers to women in the workplace trying to get another woman fired or force her to quit.

Ms. Hodsden started her studies at Kean College. She was the first TKE (Tau Kappa Epsilon) sweetheart of the Tau Lambda Chapter. She subsequently transferred to Rider University, where she founded and became President of the Le Cercle Français, the Rider University French Club. She was also a member of the International French Society.

As an undergrad, Ms. Hodsden spent a year studying abroad in Besancon, France, where she travelled extensively throughout Europe to Italy, Denmark, Germany, Sweden, and Switzerland. Upon graduating, she obtained a one year English assistant job in Limoges, France. She spent more time travelling throughout Europe to Spain, Belgium, Austria, and England.

Ms. Hodsden has a BA from Rider University in French/ESL/Secondary Education. She has a Masters in French from Middlebury College. She has a Masters in Human Resource Management from College St. Elizabeth. She obtained her PHR (Professional Human Resource) certificate in 2014, her SHRM-CP (Society Human Resources Management –Certified Professional) in 2015, and her GBA (Group Benefits Associate) from the International Foundation of Employee Benefits in 2018.

Ms. Hodsden has been a member of SHRM since 2007. She served as the Program Chair for the Howard County SHRM chapter and was on the marketing committee for the Baltimore County SHRM chapter. She currently is a board member of the North Jersey International Society of Certified Employee Benefit Specialists.

Ms. Hodsden is currently working on several other books and looks forward to publishing them in the future. She enjoys writing books about real life situations. Her favorite topics to write about are overlooked subjects she feels strongly about.

Ms. Hodsden describes herself as a vegan, feminist, socialist. She is single and currently resides in New Jersey with her 3 cats and Pontiac Firebird.

Made in the USA
Monee, IL
01 July 2020